Ed:
compliments.

Missing Caroline

A Journey Without GPS

You will have a glimpse of what I have gone through since 2007.

Hank Cunningham Dec 10/2020

Hank Cunningham
Kathleen Ratcliff
Valerie Rother

Missing Caroline

All net proceeds from the sales of this book will be donated to The Caroline Cunningham Endowment For Epilepsy at Toronto SicKKids Hospital.

tellwell

Tellwell Talent
www.tellwell.ca

ISBN
978-0-2288-2921-8 (Hardcover)
978-0-2288-2920-1 (Paperback)
978-0-2288-2922-5 (eBook)

This book is dedicated to the memory of Caroline Cunningham.

April 4, 1975 - April 8, 2007

Table of Contents

Acknowledgments

Writing this book has been extremely personal; not only is it my eulogy to Caroline, but it also represents a milestone in my healing process.

Nevertheless, there are many individuals who have contributed directly or indirectly to this work. My daughter Valerie and her mother Kathleen have made direct contributions to the body of the book. Valerie has also helped with some important recollections. Caroline's roommate Tannis delivered a magnificent eulogy contained herein, and a fellow Bishop's University classmate Kirsty Robertson also delivered a wonderful tribute.

My long-term mentor and friend, J. Lyman MacInnis, was warmly persistent in encouraging me to finish this book and he furnished the title as well. He was also instrumental in pushing me to finish my first book, edited brilliantly by his son Alan.

Friends are so important. I am so fortunate to have three great friends who have stood by me through these challenging years: Debra Hewson, Jeremy Fleming, and Stephen Reid.

Lastly, I need to acknowledge the legions of Caroline's friends. Not only are there too many to name, but they know who they are. I dare not run the risk of omitting a single name.

Caroline Cunningham

CareAlive Logo

Note her initials on the wing.

Preface

This is a personal story about the Cunningham family. Hank Cunningham and Kathleen Cunningham were married for eighteen years and produced two beautiful children: Caroline, born April 4, 1975 in Montreal, and Valerie, born December 9, 1979 in Winnipeg.

Kathleen remarried, to Bill Ratcliff.

I have not remarried.

Valerie married Vincent Rother in 2012 and they have a beautiful daughter, Charlie Jessica Rother, who was born on November 20, 2013.

Caroline never married. She died on April 8, 2007.

While I have written most of this book and the narrator's voice is mine, Kathleen and Valerie have each made significant contributions which are acknowledged herein.

This book is written primarily as a eulogy to Caroline. In addition, I write for those of you who have lost a child or children in hopes that my experience can help you understand your journey, how to deal with grief, and how to move on.

Introduction

Caroline Cunningham died on April 8, 2007. She was thirty-two. She died following a seizure from something called "SUDEP" (Sudden Unexpected Death in Epilepsy). We had never heard that term and had no idea what it meant. From the awkward name, one can glean that it was something mysterious and inexplicable. (See Appendix B for a comprehensive analysis of SUDEP written by my great friend Kimberley Berman, who joined the Care-Alive Board and made significant contributions to our foundation.)

Many families fly apart after such a tragedy. Divorces ensue; drug and alcohol abuse becomes commonplace with those involved drifting through life or committing suicide.

This did not happen to us. United by our great love for this extraordinary person, we went on to ensure that she would never be forgotten.

This is a book about grieving and healing. It is about Caroline, her loving family, and her myriad of diverse friends.

I am writing this book because I can. It has been thirteen years since my beloved daughter Caroline died. I now find myself sufficiently healed to be able to write about her life, the journey I have taken since, as well the journeys of my family: her mother Kathleen, her sister Valerie, siblings, cousins, nieces, and countless friends.

As the title suggests, there is no guidance or map for this journey; I had to find my own way in uncharted territory. While I might have made some wrong turns, encountered dead ends, and made some mistakes, I have found my way to where I am today: in a strong state of mind, healthy, and sane. I, like the rest of the Cunninghams, am a survivor: a product of typically stubborn and tough Scottish ancestors.

This journey is experienced by anyone who has lost a child; only those of us on this journey know exactly what it is like, and we alone can properly commiserate with each other. We take different routes on this journey, some of which end badly or in misery. Besides recounting my own voyage because I want to, I fervently hope that some of what I write will be of assistance to those of you who have just set out on this same tragic journey.

Not a day goes by that I do not think about Caroline. While my psyche has healed to the extent that I can write and talk about her, it still hurts and my emotions are at all times close to the surface.

There is no doubt that her death has changed me. I am not the same man. There is a big piece missing from my life. It has definitely and adversely affected my personal life. Sadness hangs over me constantly. There is a spark missing, yet I have managed to keep myself together. I have rallied my family and CC's friends, keeping everyone together while honouring Caroline at the same time.

I have ensured she will never be forgotten in a number of different ways: memorials; tree plantings; a charitable foundation by the name of Care-Alive, the Caroline Cunningham Foundation for Epilepsy (I will use Care-Alive throughout this book); an endowment at Toronto SickKids; a drop-in centre for teens with epilepsy; opening the TSX on Purple Day; one-hundred-kilometre charity bike rides; saving lives; and helping children. She loved children, and when she decided that she would not have any of her own, she became "Auntie Caroline" to her friends' children. She would have been the best aunt of all to Valerie's precocious daughter, Charlie.

What follows is my tribute to Caroline, in effect my eulogy to her. I was too emotion-stricken to be able to speak at the time of her service. I have eulogized my mother and my sister Mary, and so it is now time to pay proper tribute to Caroline.

Chapter 1

Who was she?

"I see her light everywhere
Teardrops in the sand
Smiles that light up every face and room
Friend to all
Giving without expecting anything back
Dancing, always dancing!"

We believe that Caroline wrote this herself, as writing this type of a poem was her way of doodling!

The following magnificent eulogy was delivered by Caroline's roommate Tannis Kynoch at the service:

First off, I'd like to thank Caroline's family - Hank, Kathleen, and Valerie - for bringing her into this world, for raising her to be the person she was, for sharing her with all of us, and for giving me the opportunity to share my thoughts and feelings about her with you today.

If Doreen had said that Caroline's best friend is coming up to speak to you now, approximately two dozen people would have walked up here - and they would not have been wrong. CC had such a tremendous capacity for love, such a generous heart; she always made you feel as though you were the most intelligent, the funniest, the kindest, and the most fantastic person she had ever met. She made everyone feel that they were her favourite.

She literally treasured her friends – always making sure you knew how much you were loved. She looked after her friends like diamonds, polishing them every day. Ethically-mined diamonds that she polished every day.

Even when you know CC and you know that it is impossible not to love her, impossible to miss her in a crowd, impossible not to be her friend, it is still mind-boggling to try to wrap your head around the number of people with whom she developed and grew close relationships. The number of people she loved and who loved her right back is astonishing.

It's hard to understand, even for me, and I watched her in action every day, how she managed to do this, but I think I've got some insight from the way in which we became friends. I was introduced to Caroline by our mutual and dear friend, Jane Varghese, and I would see her periodically at events Jane had organized. While I was of course drawn to her – you can't not be – we would have more accurately been described as acquaintances rather than friends for the first year that I knew her, until one day, when Jane sent a group of her friends an email with an informational form to complete. The form asked questions like "What's under your bed?" and "What's your motto?", and it asked you to list various favourites. Jane also had to put in who was the least likely to complete the form and she wrote my name down. And she was right to do so. I never would have done it otherwise, but the gauntlet had been laid down, so I completed the form including listing my favourite movies: Bringing up Baby, The Philadelphia Story, The Maltese Falcon, and The Princess Bride.

Now those first two movies are from the late 1930s and I hadn't met a lot of people who had ever heard of them, despite the fact that they starred the great Katharine Hepburn. So, I was surprised when I received an email from Caroline – who I really barely knew – the day after I emailed my responses.

And here is that email:

From: Caroline Cunningham
Sent: Monday, February 26, 2001 6:03 PM
To: Tannis Kynoch
Subject: RE: Info Thing

"tannis!!! how are ya crazykid? i just had to write and share the fact that I love your taste in films & i just taped philadelphia story on tvo on Saturday...I'm so excited!!!...i may have an unhealthy obsession for spencer tracy, cary grant and katharine hepburn but i don't care!!! they are fabulous, no one compares....movie buff to movie buff, we know it's true...ok, long day at work, no brain cells left but you are cool, end of story.

xoxo cc"

And that, I think is part of her secret, to just reach out to people without any fear of rejection, without I think, even considering that rejection ever could be possible. I could have just as easily said "Who is this?" after I got her email, but obviously that's not what happened – I emailed her right back, thrilled to have found someone who shared my excellent taste in films.

From then on, we exchanged emails on a daily basis and saw one another regularly. Although there's little that's "regular" about an activity involving Caroline, we enjoyed things like singing our hearts out at the Singalong Sound of Music, Belly Dancing at the Sultan's Tent, and attending movies, plays, and concerts in record-breaking numbers.

Even though our friendship was on solid ground, I'm still amazed at how Caroline would reach out to you to grow the relationship. I can still hear her asking me, "Tan, will you be my hot docs and film festival friend and buy passes with me? No one else will commit to that, will you commit to that?" "No" never even occurred to me.

Since 2001 we have been movie friends, trips to New York for Broadway shows friends, co-party planners with her on invitations and decorations and me on food, book club friends, dodgeball and soccer teammates, and for the last three years we've been roommates.

There is always a risk that living together will damage or end a friendship and we wanted to make sure that didn't happen, so we talked about it and realized that most people fought over bathrooms and cleaning. So we found an apartment with two bathrooms and got a cleaning lady.

And we sort of met in the middle about everything else – and while this is not to say that CC cleaned, cooked, or did her dishes on a regular basis – none of that ever mattered to me. While she did things that should have been annoying – and I know you all know what I mean – she was late for everything, she could never decide what to order in a restaurant, she often didn't even look at the menu, and at times she was almost unbelievably impractical, I found that I was simply incapable of being angry with her. I remember her once throwing a piece of food that had fallen on her lap onto the floor – at home! I reminded her, "You live here, that's our floor," but I also know that I laughed as I said it.

And I have an idea about why that might be: during the film festival one year, CC and I had lined up to get rush tickets for a film with three of my friends – one of whom had never met her before. We got in line an hour and half before the movie was supposed to start, and after we had been in the lineup for about an hour, a film festival shuttle bus came to transport people to other theatres. Despite the fact that we were third in line and our chances to get tickets for the film looked good, it was apparent to all of us by the look on her face – even my friend who had just met her – that she wanted on that bus. And it would have been so like her to change her mind and just hop on the bus to see where it would take her. No one is as spontaneous and adventure-loving as she is, so of course the rest of us wanted to stay in the lineup. One of my friends kept whispering to me, "I'm afraid that Caroline's going to get on that bus," so he ever so gently held her arm while he talked to her in an attempt to distract her from the bus. She did become distracted from the bus by the sight of her friend Desiree walking up the sidewalk towards us. Desiree and Caroline worked together and saw one another every day, but when they saw one another unexpectedly they were so delighted that they screamed out each other's names and Caroline broke free from her guard to run down the sidewalk to Des. The film lineup was on the sidewalk and it was so crowded that it was hard for them to move through the crowd quickly so they each stepped out on to the street – Yonge Street in downtown Toronto – and ran towards each other with open arms like a scene from a movie, all the while laughing and calling out to each other. When they met, they leapt into one another's arms and held each other, laughing and talking. Behind them was a cab, with the driver honking his horn as cars began to pile up behind his. Neither Caroline nor Desiree noticed the honking of the horns, and we were all laughing so hard that none of us could tell them to get off the street. Eventually the cars were all forced to drive around them.

And that's what it was like to be with Caroline: when you were with her you never noticed the honking horns, the dishes in the sink, or the perpetual lateness because all you could think of was holding her in your arms and laughing.

In all the time I've known her, Caroline and I never had a fight, which is rare for friends and unheard of for people who live together. My relationship with her is the only one in which I can say that I have no regrets. We treated one another with respect and kindness, loved one another as best we could, and I know that I did everything I could for her right to the very end. I have not yet begun to even try to comprehend what my life will be like without her in it, but I know that she would not want anyone who loved her to despair. She lived her life 100% full-on all the time, on her own terms and with a passion for what she believed in. She always did what she loved and she made sure that those around her knew that they were loved – both lessons that I hope to learn from her.

Because CC was perhaps one of the silliest people I've ever known, I don't want to end this on a sad note; so, I'd like to share some of my fun memories of her with you.

> *I will always remember her at book club, vehemently arguing her point of view about a book she'd only read twenty pages of.*
>
> *I will remember her insisting that not only was it safe, but that she should because that's what convertibles were made for – stand up in the car and wave her arms through the air, as we drove along the Danforth in the back of my sister's convertible.*
>
> *I will remember her one-liner emails that said:*
>
> - *"what's fun tonight, miss?"*
> - *"some asswipe just outbid me on eBay"*
> - *and "I just reread that - hilarious!"*
>
> *I also remember how excited she would get about the idea of, and how she longed for, a snow day: an unexpected day off – a gift if you will.*
>
> *One particular "Caroline Moment" came during a Golden Globes party when a mini-series about Hitler kept winning awards. Caroline was getting frustrated because she wanted other actors to win. Upon hearing that Hitler show win yet another award, she blurted*

> *out, "What's this with Hitler winning everything? I mean, I love him too, but come on!"*
>
> *Everyone will remember her dislike of space and aliens, and her disbelief in calories - not just in counting calories but in the actual existence of calories themselves. I remember once standing in line with her at New York Fries and she told me she was getting the salad. "New York Fries has salad?" I asked. "Yes," she said. "French fries with cheese sauce but it has tomatoes and green onions on top so I call it salad - Fries salad."*

I could talk forever about our darling girl, but then so could we all. So I'll close with a message to Caroline herself - I love you, I miss you, and I thank you for all that you brought to my life.

Tannis Kynoch
April 14th, 2007

Caroline Cunningham was born on Friday, April 4, 1975 at the Montreal General Hospital. She weighed seven pounds, three ounces, and she got an almost-perfect APGAR score.

Kathleen and I had long discussed the subject of prepared childbirth. Someone told us about a woman named Valmai Elkins, an Australian, who had introduced the Lamaze method of prepared childbirth to North America. We were intrigued and impressed. As luck would have it, there was a group of U.S. doctors practicing out of the Montreal General who subscribed to Valmai's approach. These were the days well before birthing rooms and home deliveries and the return of midwives. I became the midwife. Maternity wings were located in general hospitals and accorded no special treatment, as if pregnancy were a disease. So, we took Valmai's entire series of classes and Kathleen chose one of the doctors. Besides all the instructions regarding the pregnancy itself, Valmai took us on a tour of the hospital. She stressed a few things: 1. Montreal General was a teaching hospital, so we could expect visiting classes; 2. We would be left alone for long periods of time as our doctor would not arrive until it was almost birth time; 3. This meant that we would be in the hands of an intern who had considerable power. Valmai warned us not to argue with or otherwise upset the intern, as I would then be forced to leave the hospital. As you will see, this was sound advice.

On April 3, 1975, Montreal experienced a huge end-of-winter snowstorm with accompanying high winds. We lived in Mont St. Hilaire, twenty-five miles east of Montreal.

The contractions began, no doubt brought on by the low-pressure system. The winds howled all night. As the snow piled up and the drifts grew, I began to wonder what we were to do. Perhaps it would be a home birth or perhaps we could get a helicopter ride. Anyway, as dawn broke and the storm was ebbing, the contractions were coming closer but still not strong enough and her water had not broken. We made our decision. I remembered that there was a commuter train in the morning. CNR had left the train at St. Hyacinthe the night before; thus, I knew that it would be going into Montreal. I confirmed this with CNR. Then, after reaching her doctor, he advised us to come to the city and get a hotel room until labour was more advanced. I phoned the Queen Elizabeth hotel and, because of the storm, they were fully booked. I explained our situation and voilà – they found us a room!

Getting to the train station was another adventure. We drove a Volkswagen Beetle in those days and it proved to be OK in the snow. The train station (platform really) at Otterburn Park was at the bottom of the hill beside the river. We surfed downhill to the station and got on the train with Kathleen in labour and wearing a gigantic mink coat. Several of my friends from St. James Street (the Montreal equivalent to Bay Street) were also on the train so it was quite the trip as Kathleen was breathing hard while I chatted with my bond trader friends. They were appropriately respectful.

We made it to the hotel and whiled away the time doing crossword puzzles and a little shopping. By four in the afternoon, we reached her doctor and he recommended that we be admitted to the hospital. By then, it was a beautiful spring day with the sun shining and the snow melting.

We checked in and were ushered into a labour room. We met the intern and explained that we were planning to use the Lamaze technique and that I was going to be there for the entire duration. This was early, practically pioneer, days for Lamaze. This intern did not like it at all and we did not like his negative attitude. Summoning all my diplomatic skills, which had been drilled into me by Valmai, I politely requested to see the resident doctor who was in charge of the maternity floor. Those who know me realize that this was not in my normal character! I have never been known for my patience or tact!

I explained the situation gently and respectfully and requested a change of interns. He did that and we carried on with a more positive intern. Yes, we were left alone for long periods of time and yes, there were small classes of students who dropped in.

Finally, they broke Kathleen's water (I think that I did it!) and took us to the delivery room. I was there as her coach to help her with her breathing and to provide support. She wanted a natural childbirth but, as the pain became unbearable, she began swearing like a trooper and asking for an epidural. It was too late so she toughed it out and at ten fifteen p.m., Caroline came into the world. She was alert and cried immediately. Her eyes were clear and blue; we were determined that she would be born drug-free. Her APGAR score was almost perfect. I felt this enormous swelling of love and pride to witness the birth of this special child. The doctor looked over at me and asked: "Mr. Cunningham, would you like to cut the umbilical cord?"

Yikes, I thought. I told him to show me the dotted line. I cut her umbilical cord; this was a special and unique moment. After doing that, and since they were attending to Kathleen, they were looking for someone to hold Caroline. I quickly volunteered and was thus the first person to hold her. I believe strongly that eye contact is important.

A note about her name: we had thought she would be called April or Diana. Caroline was third on the list, but as soon as we saw her, we knew Caroline was the right name. It is lyrical and bilingual. Owing to the length of her name in addition to my surname, we did not give her a middle name.

Kathleen's parents, Ed and Beryl McCullough, lived in Montreal, Dorval actually, while my parents were in Alberta. Thus, we spent more time with Ed and Beryl who doted on Caroline. She was the first grandchild for Kathleen's parents and they were over the moon with happiness. My parents already had grandchildren so they were not as excited. I was, though.

Later, after getting Kathleen back to her room and Caroline to the maternity room, I went out to celebrate. As I could not stand smoking, there was no way I was going to have a cigar. Rather, I went to Ben's Delicatessen, sat at a counter stool, and had a banana split. Years later, I brought Caroline and Valerie to that exact spot and relived the occasion.

It turned out that we were fortunate to have Caroline born on the Friday. The intense low-pressure system resulted in a record amount of births in the following seventy-two hours with patients filling up the hallways!

It was exciting for us to be the parents to this beautiful baby. Kathleen breastfed her for many months. Caroline was always happy, despite the odd case of colic. The demands of motherhood are significant, so I sent Kathleen away for a week at a time to recharge. I loved taking care of Caroline and I think it helped me to bond tighter with her. Always curious, she began to exhibit a strain of stubbornness common to the Cunninghams! She cut her cheek one day and refused to keep the butterfly bandage on (she was too young for stitches). Thus, she grew up with a small crescent-shaped scar. In a prelude to her adult life, she displayed an above-average level of empathy and generosity. She was also quick on the uptake!

I remember her as a toddler on Brentwood Ave. in Beaconsfield; she always attracted the young boys on the street. She had a sunny disposition and everyone liked her. I remember she was wicked funny even in those early days; one day she demonstrated being klutzy on purpose and deliberately messed up on her cross-country skis.

She was a good athlete. From the earliest time, she excelled in soccer, and this culminated in her making the Oakville Rep team, a significant achievement as Oakville was a national hotbed for soccer. One time when she was playing house league, her team was getting beaten badly. She got annoyed and took the ball from one end of the field to the other and scored with her left foot! This came as no surprise to me as I had seen her do it before, but it was still a great goal! However, it totally fooled the goalkeeper. Like most goalies, she was used to players using their dominant foot.

We joined the Oakville Club where she once again excelled, this time in both badminton and tennis. She competed but did not care much if she won or lost. In tennis, she had a great serve (when it went in!) and a thunderbolt forehand which I could sometimes not return! It was all or nothing with her! I enjoyed playing tennis with her. While she could be competitive, she mostly liked to play. She never lost her temper or cool. She merely enjoyed herself with little regard for the score. Winning was not the only thing.

We played some badminton together. She and Valerie were both terrific badminton players.

Another achievement of hers of which I am proud is that she became fluent in French. We moved to Winnipeg in 1979 when she was four. The immersion program in Winnipeg was first-rate. The only classes she took in English were English classes! This ultimately helped her in business as she was the go-to person when dealing with French clients and associates. At one point, GMP Capital (her employer for seven-and-a-half years) tried to convince her to move to Montreal, but she was not interested.

She was an excellent student and possessed a beautiful mind. Her marks were in the nineties typically. They slid somewhat towards her Grade 13 graduation and I believe that our divorce weighed heavily on her mental state. Her marks were slightly too low for her first choice, Guelph University. She then opted for Bishop's University in Lennoxville, Quebec, where she studied political science. She was a prolific and talented writer; there is little doubt that she would have had some of her literary efforts published. While at Bishop's, she had a roaring good time for the most part, but her marks began to suffer when she lost her two beloved grandmothers in the space of three months. She never got her degree, just missing one credit which she never acquired. From there she went on to begin her career on Bay Street.

Her Life Goals

- To remain, over the course of my life, fairly physically fit
- To keep challenges in my life
- To marry a man that I adore and who adores me
- To travel and see this wonderful planet – the good and the bad
- To travel to an area that is not blessed with hope like Canada is and make a difference in a person's life who has lost hope
- To get a piece of my writing published, whether it be a segment in a magazine, in a collection, my own book of fiction, or my non-fiction account of the state of something
- To act in a movie or a television with an actor or an actress I have admired for a long time
- To win an Oscar or a literary award from peers
- To research astrology

- To have children and to raise them to have open minds
- To live in a city and in the country
- To study journalism at university along with broadening my knowledge in other areas (psychology, Spanish)
- To be a journalist with integrity and one who gains respect by covering important happenings and issues
- To learn to ski without breaking a bone, in my middle age.
- To read all the books and see all the videos I never had time to devote to
- To keep in touch with old friends and surround myself with an eclectic group of good-hearted, enthusiastic, eccentric, open-minded people
- To be by the ocean

Kathleen unearthed this from Caroline's papers. She wrote this when she was twenty or so while at Bishop's.

CC could have accomplished almost this entire list. I am certain that she would have published some of her writings and also become an actor. After being diagnosed with epilepsy at age twenty-six, she learned that it would be risky to have children as she would have had to go off her meds for the pregnancy or else risk birth defects. She abandoned the marriage idea, though there was no lack of suitors! She went on to spread joy wherever she went and cultivate a wonderful network of friends. She was an excellent writer and actor. In this book I include many examples of her writing. She had a vivid imagination and could write in English in addition to French! There is little doubt that she would have become a published author. With her love of children, I am certain she would have written amazing books for children. Here are some poems she wrote while at Bishop's University:

Uninvited

On the fringes, self-aware
Clamouring to break in but
Shielded by cold stares and
Empty glances
Why have I
Been chosen as this soul
To be toyed with?
Invited, then shunned

In a world that begs
For the answers I have
Somewhere.
Caroline Cunningham

Salt-Stained

The tears taste good.
Taste like pain
Swallowed whole,
As I let them trickle
Onto my lips before
I wipe them away.
The liquid remnants
Crystallize like
Thoughts and stain
My freckled cheek
As a cruel reminder.
I only hope today
I can keep them at bay

Twenty-two

Someone who'll wipe the
Tears from my cheek
And make it real.
This is what comes to mind
As my eyes close and
My lips purse to snuff
Out twenty-two candles on a cake before me.

While these examples may sound serious or sad, I am advised by CC's fellow Bishop's grad and close friend, Kirsty Robertson, that these were written mostly tongue in cheek. Caroline had a wicked sense of humour. She recalls Caroline standing on the stove and reading these at top volume!

She also became a stand-up comedian after progressing steadily through five Second City seasons. She was convinced and determined that her talents would land her acting roles, perhaps comedic.

She had a paid summer off in 2000 and travelled to Australia with her great friend (yes, another one) Evita Strobel. She penned the following email to Tannis, her roommate:

Sent: Thursday, July 20 2000
Subject: No worries

Hello Crazy Cats, or Mates as they say, one quick message before I leave the land down under...thanks to all who have written me, it's been great to check in with the homeland... as you may be able to tell, I've had just an amazing time...Sydney, Alice Springs, Ayers Rock, Darwin, Kakadu National Park, in the " Top End" bush country, and the coastal Cairns/Daintree/Great Barrier Reef area... yesterday, we hiked through a 110-year-old rainforest, the Daintree World Heritage Rain Forest and Cape Tribulation, just north of Cairns (Cans!) on the East Coast... amazing wildlife-spotting: tree kangaroos, saw some grouse, bright blue butterflies, so many birds, a few turtles; it was so peaceful... later in the afternoon we took a tour over the Tablelands (farming and wildlife plateau inland from Cairns) and swam in a few waterfalls and went platypus-spotting... so cute! As part of the international songfest on the tour bus I most likely completely embarrassed myself (although the crowd seemed to be into it) by reciting/singing/yelling the Molson "I am Canadian" spiel and got audience participation in between each line by having Dutch, Germans, Brits (Poms as they are called here), American! Irish, Scottish, Aussie, and Japanese shouting "I AM CANADIAN" while I shouted out things like "We wear tuques, not hats!", "We eat maple syrup, not Aunt Jemima!", and "we drink BEER, not watered-down piss!!..." The Americans were very jovial about it... Melissa, you would have loved it!!... Well, the trip has been an exercise in complete sleep deprivation, but worth every eye-opening minute (Prague 2000 crew I know you feel my pain!). Most tours leave at 5 or 6 a.m. and we had one flight at 5:35, loving that airport shuttle at 3:35 a.m.... I hear you laughing at me from here... I only almost missed one tour, when we were off to Ayers rock at 6:30 (I was getting a bit soft at this point; we'd slept till 8:30 the previous day)... camping at Kakadu National Park was awesome, had a 4-a.m.er there... and apparently you can't sleep in a four-wheel drive while going through creeks sitting sideways even if you rock-climbed for five hours and swam in crocodile-infested (no jokes!) danger waters... I reckon I'm Crocodile Dundette by now... no worries... well, I had a great snorkel/scuba off the Great Barrier reef a few days ago and I was screwed because I couldn't say WOW or laugh underwater without gagging and choking... even with asthma it was fun, such bright colours... saw eight barracuda altogether (very beady eyes), held many sea cucumbers, saw a moray eel and so many schools of pink/blue/purple/yellow fish... just north of Cairns we also stayed at a hostel that had canopy-covered cabins right in the middle of the rainforest, which was amazing, and a few green tree frogs fell onto the roof during the night... could see them against the moonlight! The whole trip is catching up to us now and we fell asleep at 9:30 last night and slept in until... coulda done 9:30 but the French girls in our room woke up at 7 and proceeded to rustle ten or eleven plastic bags, pack, and re-pack about five times and generally wake us up (although the sleeping mask is my new best friend, so that helped a bit)... we fly today at 5:40 p.m. (Thurs) and Evita gets off in Brisbane (Wendy, I am still working on that card...!) and I continue on to Sydney and I fly to Toronto at 9-something a.m. from there... I believe I may treat myself to a stay at an airport hotel and enjoy a bath and some TV... Hey, I'll throw it on Visa; there's plenty of room. Ha! Well, it's obvious that I'm rambling; I have many stories to tell when I return home. I will see the nbfinancial-ers on Monday, and everyone else: I hope to see you soon! Could someone please email this to Korinna at her new job, I don't have the address yet, many thanks! Also, Natty Gan, I'm getting home at 5 p.m. on Friday and I would love you forever if you'd pick me up at around 7 to head out to K's cottage...the fun never stops!! Thanks to everyone who encouraged me to go on this trip; it has refreshed me, challenged me, and I've met so many amazing people to keep in touch with... your support, as always, means the world to me... can't wait to get back and pay this trip off!!

Love and hugs,
CC Down Undah
Xoxoxoxoxoxoxoxo

P.S. I'll be checking my mail one more time before I leave Sydney Friday morning at 8 a.m. (6 p.m. Thurs for you, I think... I'm all confused).

Caroline lived her daily life to the max. Her own birthday parties were legendary, never just lasting for one day. Valerie thought that she knew her sister and her friends well until one celebratory evening at Reservoir Lounge, a live jazz club on Wellington Street. Valerie knew the first twenty or so friends who arrived but not the next thirty or so!!!

CC loved Christmas. By the way, her nickname CC just happened naturally, especially considering she had no middle name. It seemed to suit her personality as well. She wrote individual cards to everyone and took great pains to wrap each "prezzie." For several consecutive Christmas Eves, the girls drove to Hastings and we went out and cut down our very own tree from my property and then decorated it. She treasured her prezzies but got more joy out of her gifts to others, carefully choosing them and wrapping them herself.

We would have friends and family over and there were some competitive crokinole tournaments played! We also played Trivial Pursuit and Clue to name a couple more. Try as they might, they could not best me in Trivial Pursuit, owing primarily to my massive knowledge of sports trivia.

Christmas would never be the same after April 8, 2007. I had zero interest in celebrating it. One year I went to Las Vegas; other years I did nothing.

It was not until Charlie arrived that I began to take part in Christmas. Thanksgiving became a favourite time of year, but Easter remained and remains nothing but sadness.

I do remember some fun Easters. My fondest memory, and I remember doing this for several years, was to hold Easter egg hunts. Typically, I would put clues in the form of a crossword puzzle which would send the girls all over the house. At my farm, I was sure to send them over big distances. Meanwhile, the big treasure was sitting under my chair! The girls always enjoyed this. I have now resurrected the Easter egg hunt with Charlie, and she too just loves the hunt!

The African Adventure

CC loved to travel and I will chronicle her adventures. It was her dream to spend a month in Africa and she booked it. She wanted to take pictures and, in true Caroline-retro-fashion, she bought a new **film** camera and, with my urging, she bought a good zoom lens. Four days before her departure, she called and asked me to help her with her camera. She had not even taken it out of the box!

She came to my condo and, after charging the battery, I gave her some simple advice.

As film was cheap, I told her to shoot often and be ready to shoot at all times. I made her load the film herself and then I took her out into downtown Toronto where I told her to treat cars and people like animals, either panning for action or composing stills. She took some good pics that night. This preparation paid off as she took some great pics that her fellow travellers missed.

From Africa

Her mother was not keen on her going to Africa. With epilepsy, Caroline had to take many more inoculations than the typical traveller. After a few days in Africa, she emailed Kathleen: "Guess what, Mom. No malaria yet!" Her mother was strongly opposed to her going on this trip but Caroline, in her stubborn nature, would not listen and felt compelled to josh her mother.

Here is her first email:
August 15, 2005

Hello everyone!! Jambo! I am alive and loving life in East Africa, if I could only describe how difficult it is to send an email/fid access. We are so remote here. I am very cut off and it actually feels very liberating... I had typed a long email to everyone two days ago and it got erased and it was a little heartbreaking... so this is just to say hi and it is a victory if it goes through!! The group and I are in Kisii on our way to Lake Victoria in Western Kenya and having an amazing time... this is the only time we won't be partaking in Kenya's local beer, Tusker, as we are staying at a Catholic Mission, and camping near the lake tomorrow which is supposed to be beautiful... on our way past the Kenya/ Tanzania border, then to the Serengeti. Yesterday, saw many rhinos, baboons, and a lake full of flamingos and pelicans at Lake Nakuru. Africa is truly beautiful and I'm with a great group of Dutch people – all between the ages of seventeen and thirty-five with one father and his two daughters. We are having a blast, staying in some bandas (thatched roof huts) and mostly camping in breathtaking spots. At Lake Baringo, we took a boat ride to see hippos, crocs, yellow-billed storks, and fish eagles... and then we heard hippos on land outside our tents that night, good times! Got up at 6 a.m. for a hike into a Maasai village. The people are so friendly and amazing. I miss you all and hope you are all well...

love,
CC on Safari
Next email:
August 22, 2005
Subject: Serengeti Lions and Tusker Beer!!

Hey all!!! No malaria yet and I have never used so much DEET and Purell in my life... but that being said, this is the most beautiful part of the world I have ever been...

Since my last email, we've seen so much more wildlife... a pride of male lions in Serengeti and two cheetahs running right next to our truck, a leopard in a tree, two hundred zebras, an elephant, and her baby. We saw the big five: Lions, elephants, rhinos, hippos, and cheetahs [*Hank:* She had the worst luck at spotting deer at my farm, even if five of them were standing still!] *on our first game drive here in Samburu National Park two weeks ago and it's only gotten better. We took 4wd vehicles down to the Ngorongoro Crater where there is a large concentration of wildlife and actually saw a kill!!!! A large buffalo that was already limping tried to attack a lion he thought was on its own, but actually there were six or seven lions lurking around nearby and these lions just pounced and attacked the large buffalo. You could feel it in the air that something was about to happen. Hundreds of zebras were fleeing the area and it was quite a sight. We photographed it and just sat back and watched nature happen for about twenty minutes, incredible! I LOVE my camera! I've had dust on the lens that can't be removed for about ten days now; it's insane. We travel in a large overland truck, usually with the windows strapped open; they zip up and down depending if we are on a game drive or not. We're very high up so can see everything; it's great! It fits twenty people and everyone is a lot of fun... our guide Jeannine is great, and bilingual (Dutch/English) – Tusker, the Kenyan beer, has been consumed every night by the fire. I cooked spaghetti Bolognese over coals with Nick, our chef, last night and we made some traditional Kenyan food, Ugali, the other night, but he cooks every night. We've been out for dinner a couple of nights.*

P.S. I've gone through eighteen films; it's crazy. I really hope there isn't a huge piece of black dust on each picture... I think it's just in the viewfinder. Really, I hope!

We are in Arusha right now, probably Tanzania's third biggest city, for lunch on the way to Moshi. We leave our driver and chef tonight and tomorrow take a bus to Dar-es-Salaam where we catch the ferry to Zanzibar for the last four days of our trip... the most relaxing four days, in a beachfront hotel. I love you lots and miss you all. Thanks for all the emails... it means a lot:)

I will probably be able to write a lot more on Zanzibar.

Love,
CC on Safari
xxxxxx

She went on this trip with fifteen people from Holland. Typical of Caroline, this just happened, with friend Theresa Vanderpost's help. I remember asking CC how she managed to travel with these people, who all spoke English, but who spoke Dutch amongst themselves. In typical CC-style, she told me that she would spend a day one-on-one with each person!

During her vacation, she spent a day volunteering by befriending a young boy with epilepsy who had been abandoned by his family. She loved the native people and they loved her.

Generosity

Caroline gave freely to all her diverse friends, in an open and loving fashion, never looking for anything in return. Whether planning parties, taking care of children, or just plain being there, she added so much fun and value.

Along with a colleague from GMP, she co-founded the Bay Street Stampede and it was successful in raising significant funds for charitable organizations. After seeing the good work done by *Right To Play* in Africa, she adopted it and told us to give them money in lieu of gifts for her. She was a stalwart volunteer at TIFF for years, along with Tannis. Finally, she decided to concentrate on attending TIFF and had many wonderful years doing that. The Oscars might have been her favourite event and she was notorious for organizing theme parties with contests.

Caroline had an empathetic streak seen in very few people. She judged no one, treating each friend as a person, without regard to race, creed, religion, gender, age, or sexual orientation.

On the surface, she appeared to be loosey-goosey, but in reality, she was a perfectionist who would always finish something properly. She worked hard too and would always go the extra mile to see a task through to the end, whether it be hers or a colleague's. Some of us had to wait for her on many an occasion. Valerie and I had dinner with CC frequently, and we always betted on when we would get the Blackberry message saying she was on her way. (She was still in the office!)

Summary: How she lived

She was always happy; it is difficult to find a photo of her not smiling. She had an enormous stubborn streak and could stonewall anybody. No one could talk to her about epilepsy. It took a supreme effort from her great friend Desiree to get her to go to the Neurological Clinic at Toronto Western Hospital. Desiree did so out of her love for Caroline, and she was the only one of Caroline's friends able to break through the wall. She wanted Caroline to know, as well as the rest of us, if she had had any previous trauma to her brain. After two full days of testing, they found no evidence of brain trauma and judged her to be at low risk.

Valerie tried repeatedly to break through to her to little avail. Valerie fretted constantly about Caroline's tendency to only take her meds intermittently or just forget to take them. This behaviour likely caused some of her seizures. I vividly remember arriving at my condo on Christmas Eve and there was an EMS ambulance outside the building. It was Caroline and she had had a seizure right in front of Valerie. CC was adamant about not going to a hospital and tore the IV out of her arm. Typically, as long as a seizure victim did not incur any physical injury, they would recover in five or ten minutes. At first, this was a terrifying event to witness as we were afraid that she had experienced brain injury. Typically, she was disoriented for a few minutes before returning to normalcy.

She made friends with everyone and was full of love; she was a free spirit and loyal to a fault. She was a retro gal for sure, handwriting messages and cards and wrapping presents with care. She would put together fun packages for friends (and Valerie) when they needed a boost. She had legions of friends. As Malcolm Gladwell describes in *The Tipping Point,* Caroline was a Connector, at the heart of an extensive group of friends who she cultivated continually. It is a lengthy list but I would be remiss if I did not mention some of these friends: Evita Strobel (a friend from primary school who went to Australia with her; Tannis of course (her roommate and fellow TIFFER); Lindsey Clarke, who taught English in Quebec City, not far from Lennoxville, and they would party together some!; Nataly Alves, a special friend who was close to both of my daughters and who also worked for me on two occasions; and Karinna, a great travelling friend.

Finally, she was an environmentalist ahead of her time. Some of the folks at the ultra-capitalist GMP called her a "tree-hugger!" Thus, she was a peacenik too, and she was even tear-gassed at a protest rally in Quebec City for one of her causes. Should she be alive today, she would be all over global warming.

Chapter 2

Impact on Valerie

Caroline touched many, many lives in an extraordinary way, none more than her sister Valerie's:

2008 – Valerie. This was our memorial to Caroline which we published in the *Globe and Mail* on April 8.

My earliest memories about Caroline are of a big sister who was happy and playful and fun, and very loving and affectionate. I remember wanting to be exactly like her. I remember "borrowing" her clothes and following her around everywhere, and I remember insisting that I should be allowed to do whatever she did, even though I was nearly five years her junior.

I remember Caroline singing.

I remember becoming the big sister. That first phone call from the hospital where she was taken after she had mysteriously collapsed and fell down a flight of stairs. I remember hearing the word seizure for the first time and I remember dismissing it because how could she have had a seizure??? She is a healthy twenty-six-year-old with no history of seizures. I remember assuming that it was a mistake.

I remember Caroline dancing.

I remember Christmas Eve. I remember being locked out of my dad's condo building and Caroline coming to let me in. I remember that before she could open the door, she seized in front of me and there was no way to get in. I remember banging on the door with all my might, hoping to break it. I remember screaming. I remember the fear. I remember finally getting in and holding her head in my lap while other more capable people called 911. I remember how she looked up at me as the seizure ended with no recognition in her eyes; I remember thinking that she was brain-damaged, that she had hit her head too hard on the marble floor, and that she would never be the same. Witnessing a grand mal seizure is one of the most unpleasant things I can think of. I struggle very hard to forget.

I remember Caroline playing.

I remember hearing the word epilepsy for the first time and looking at the E.R. doctor like he was crazy. I remember meeting with her neurologist, and I remember him telling her that she would never have children. I remember telling her that I would have children for her. I remember the doctor telling her to take these pills and that everything would be ok. I remember that it wasn't.

I remember Caroline calling me her "little boo-boo" well into my twenties.

I don't remember how many times I rushed to various emergency rooms in a total panic. I don't remember how many fights Caroline and I had about taking her medication. I don't remember how many times I tried to talk about it with her and met a brick wall of silence. A wall that I did not realize she shared with every other epileptic around the world... I thought that it was just hers.

I remember Caroline laughing.

I remember not feeling well and asking Caroline if we could reschedule our movie date. I remember dropping her off at her apartment. I remember hugging her and telling her that I loved her. I remember the police knocking on my door four hours later. I remember freaking out. I remember looking around with hope that I just needed to go to another hospital, and I remember all the heads shaking "no." I remember that I didn't get it.

I remember Caroline hugging.

I remember that the police don't let you tell someone by phone that a loved one has died. I remember racing to Lakefield from Toronto to try and beat the police to my mother's door. I remember failing. I remembered my dad being out of town and I remember the phone call I had to make that broke his heart. I remember hugging my dad at the airport – finally having him home. I remember making all the funeral arrangements and phone calls to family and friends because I couldn't put my parents through that.

I remember Caroline giving.

I don't remember much of the next couple of months.

I remember hearing the word SUDEP. I remember reading the coroner's report.

I remember coming out of my grief stupor. I remember all the ways that I have tried to honour Caroline. I went and bought a homeless man a meal and gave him $20 because she would have. I joined her soccer team – The "CC Cosmos." I started using reusable bags at the grocery store. I started enjoying life more and working less. I travelled. These were all things that she was passionate about and it gave me great pleasure to honour her in these ways, but it wasn't enough. This is why the Caroline Cunningham Foundation exists. The terrible grief married my unstoppable desire to make it all mean something, and they became the parents of Care-Alive. To care for the living. To educate families and the public at large, to make a difference, to break down the brick walls, to save even one life. What an honour. What a responsibility. Caroline wouldn't have it any other way.

I remember Caroline.

Valerie delivered a brave and wonderful eulogy to her sister:

So, before I begin today, I'd like to thank everyone that has reached out to my family this week. The outpouring and sharing of happy memories has given us comfort when it seems impossible and we owe a special thanks to Tannis. We sincerely appreciate all that you have done and been a part of these last few days, and without you, my family would be more broken. We love you.

So when I first started thinking about speaking today I thought I had no words. But now it seems I have too many. There are, as Tannis said, a million things I could say. I could talk about Caroline's worldwide network of friends, I could talk about her large extended family that loved her just as dearly, I could talk about how many young lives she touched as her friends and family began having children, or I could talk about her many travel adventures, but I won't, not today. I truly hope that all of these stories are told later, but for now I am going to focus on what Caroline meant to me.

From the minute I was born I knew I was loved not only by my parents but by a big sister who couldn't hug me enough. Pretty much immediately I wanted to do everything she did – go everywhere she went, play with all her toys, hang out with all her friends, and of course wear all her clothes. For the most part Caroline tolerated this with the grace and understanding afforded a big sister.

Caroline was also my number one cheerleader. She never missed a single important moment in my life and always managed to be present for those not so important moments that still required an older sister's touch. Oddly we became our closest when we lived the farthest apart. She was blessed with a knack for knowing when people needed her, and especially me.

When we were both in university, a province apart, I'd be having a tough time and I would come home and miraculously a care package would show up with fun movies, candies, stickers, mixed tapes, and other funny little trinkets. This seemingly small yet incredibly generous act of kindness always erased my blues – especially because it was often followed by a two-hour phone call where we would laugh and laugh and wonder if we were the only two people in the world that loved the movie Dirty Dancing.

Caroline also protected me fiercely but always encouraged me to live my life. This was in my opinion her second-best quality, for CC was also my best friend, and for those of you today that are lucky enough to have called her a friend, you will agree that this is by far her best quality.

And so by coming here today, you may not have realized it, but you have all signed up for a new job. I am certain this is a sentiment that will be echoed by many today. But here is my take on it. You are all desperate to help and to do something, anything. You have all said it to me many times, and it took me a while, but I am here to tell you that I have thought of something perfect we can all do. We are all teachers now. Each and every one of us must go forth and demonstrate extreme kindness and generosity to all the people in our lives. Make time when it is scarce. Give money generously to causes and people, even if you haven't much to start with. Be there in an instant for a friend. Do nice things for someone who on the surface may not appear to deserve it. Embrace others for who they are, and finally, and quite frankly most importantly, we must all laugh as often and as loudly as possible. It is our job to teach friends, family, co-workers, travel agents, clients, strangers, and most especially we must pass this on to the precious children who she adored. Nothing would make her happier.

For me this is not goodbye. Goodbye would be impossible, so I have selected a poem by e. e. cummings that couldn't possibly describe my feelings any better.

I carry your heart with me
And I carry it in my heart
I am never without it
Anywhere I go you go my dear
And what ever is done by only me
Is your doing, my darling.
I fear no fate
For you are my fate my sweet
And I want no world
For beautiful, you are my world, my true.
Here is the deepest secret no one knows
Here is the root of the root
And the bud of the bud
And the sky of the sky
Of a tree called life
Which grows higher than the soul can hope
Or mind can hide
It is the wonder that is keeping the stars apart
I carry your heart
I carry it in my heart.
I love you, my sweet Caroline, and I know I will see you again one day.

Date: April 25, 2007, 10:55 46 AM
To: Hank Cunningham
from: Valerie Cunningham

"Today is much like yesterday. Crummy. I don't know how I am going to do this, Dad, and it's scary. I just don't care about anything anymore, let alone work. It just seems so pointless and I can't seem to snap out of it."

In fact, Valerie could not snap out of it. She resigned. Owing to a personal development, she was homeless as well as out of work! Valerie went through a horrible period of time, beginning in December of 2006 when she had a messy breakup. After giving notice on her apartment, she had not found another place to live when she lost Caroline. Devastated by this loss, she was a mess. At the service, her colleague Elizabeth Hermant, who had been on vacation, suggested that Valerie move in with her and her parents. Valerie said yes and she enjoyed the comfort of being around a loving family for several months. Elizabeth turned out to be a true friend, avoiding all the unnecessary and unhelpful things that most people did. Valerie heard another phrase from a former boss at the service, one that rang and rings true: "It doesn't get easier."

Eventually, after an extended leave from her job, she came back and resigned, not being able to cope. Valerie became a bartender at Vertical, the same restaurant where the reception was held after Caroline's service. It added a drink to their menu: "*The CC Cosmo – equal parts Belvedere vodka and Chambord mixed with orange juice and cranberry juice and garnished, of course, with a blackberry.*" She was a dedicated Blackberry user!

Vertical was partly-owned by some GMP people. Valerie excelled at bartending, like everything else she has ever tried. She told me that it was the ideal job, as she did not have to think or take anything home with her. She bartended for nine months or so until one day she had had enough and returned to her human resources career.

Valerie was close friends with many of Caroline's friends. On a plane back from visiting CC's tree in Central Park with Jane Varghese, yet another great friend of CC's, Jane suggested that she investigate the world of corporate HR, rather than returning to the vicious world of headhunting. One thing led to another, and over drinks with, yes, another friend, Kelly Patricio, Valerie decided to enter the corporate HR world. She landed a contract with National Bank Financial; this led to a further improvement in her condition as she knew many people there from her First Marathon summer job days. (National Bank bought First Marathon, where I had worked for twelve years.) She was surrounded by people who loved her.

Ultimately, she found a nice apartment, got a cat, and began dating the man she was going to marry: Vincent Rother.

She then landed a full-time position at CIBC Mellon and her life began to stabilize. She has made great strides in the corporate HR world since. She married Vincent Rother and is the mother of Charlie Jessica Rother, one of the most delightful children imaginable.

It was during this time that I proposed we begin a charitable foundation which Valerie, and everyone else, was in favour of. To get it launched, I did the heavy lifting and on January 1, 2009, the Caroline Cunningham Foundation for Epilepsy came into being. This rallied my family. I grew closer to Kathleen, as we shared the worst possible memory of losing our daughter. As I have chronicled somewhere else in this book, this brought us all together: Kathleen, Valerie, Tannis, my niece Rachelle (my brother Scott's daughter), and many of Caroline's friends.

Valerie threw herself into the foundation and spearheaded many of our important initiatives.

The importance of the foundation as a rallying point for CC's family ultimately supplanted our interest in the cause itself. It kept us together.

Impact on Me

I went back to work too soon and could barely function. Kim Stephany, a former girlfriend, a true friend, and the one who had volunteered to fly back with me from South Carolina, recognized this and took me away from the office on several occasions. She also invited me to share a couple of weekends at her cottage in Niagara on the Lake. All of what she did for me was with a generous heart and I remain grateful. I owe her a debt of gratitude for her constant support and friendship.

My situation affected my personal life as well. When people asked me how many children I had, and as this is almost a universal conversation starter, I would respond: "Two." Typically, this was greeted by no further questions. The odd person might ask about my daughters' names, but that would be it. It astounds me how few people scratch the surface to show actual interest. It is then that I remember how wrapped up most people are in their own world. It was easier for me to **not** talk about losing a child. When I began to date again after a considerable time, I was an emotional wreck. If I met someone where there was mutual attraction, I would wait for months before summoning the courage to tell her. Sometimes, this turned out poorly, but most women, especially mothers, understood. They also understood that they were not meeting all of me. I was a shadow of my previous self. There was a piece missing.

When I met someone who had known Caroline, they struggled to know what to say. As most of them had children, I asked them what they would do if they lost one of theirs. That usually ended the conversation but it did get the message across. No one was able to contemplate the loss of one of their children. In my role as Chairman of Care-Alive, I met several people who had lost a child and wanted to gain some perspective. Once it was a family who had lost their daughter after nine seizure-free years. I consoled the mother but, by then, her family was falling apart. A fellow Cambridge Club member lost his son a few years after Caroline died; he understood immediately that we were on a unique path together. We sought each other's company out regularly. Often, it was about listening and consoling. There was little I could offer in the way of practical advice other than outlining the stages of grief.

It was a lot like being divorced: true friends stay with you and everyone else runs away, mostly because they are unable to deal with it.

All of us (Valerie, Kathleen, Tannis, niece Rachelle, and me) have had many extrasensory perception (ESP) moments. We will see a flash of blonde hair in a crowd; we will hear her voice. I took to meditating in my forest on my farm. After sitting on a tree stump for thirty minutes or so, she would come to me (and still does), her head flying by with a pennant flying behind. She would say to me: "Dad, I am OK." This happened numerous times.

I was gobsmacked. A parent seldom thinks about losing a child. Of course, we all do but we quickly banish this unbearable thought. When I did lose Caroline, it was mind-numbing. Did I accept her death? No! Was I angry? Yes. These two statements are typical of early grief, I came to understand. Over time, the anger subsides and the acceptance level rises, but it does take time – in my case a full ten years.

The week leading up to the service was a blur. Valerie was staying with me at my condo in downtown Toronto; one day we went out for a pub lunch at the Jersey Giant. The bartender knew somehow that we were mourning but mercifully said nothing. On the way back, we went into the St. Andrew's Anglican Church and lit candles. I had never done that in my life.

I carried on; we met with the funeral people. I kept thinking what a horrible job to have but they were efficient at it. Once we indicated that she was to be cremated, they asked what we intended to do with the ashes. No one spoke. Finally, I said that I would take them. What would I like them to be contained in? They ushered us into a room where there was a staggering display of options available. By this time, Kathleen and Valerie decided, naturally, that they would like to have some ashes also. I was drawn to a rosewood clock with a round brass front and Roman numerals. They called it an "Eternity Clock." I liked it for the fact that it would be a constant reminder that time keeps moving on. I loved it and chose it. It is in my home office about six feet from where I am writing this. Kathleen chose a beautiful urn and Valerie chose a locket. Kathleen has her urn and I have my Eternity Clock. Valerie has a pendant necklace with a small amount of ashes. Kathleen also has a lock of her hair in a glass tube held in a small pewter piece of art. We want to keep her with us so we don't have to go anywhere to see her.

Cremation

Valerie in disbelief

On the date of the cremation, we had a chance to look at her one last time before the event. I could not stay long; I barely recognized her. We proceeded to the crematorium for the saddest day of our lives. When she was cremated, we knew it was final; she was not coming back.

After that, it was on to the service. You have already read the magnificent eulogies delivered by Tannis and Valerie. For all my speech-making ability, this was too much for me and I had the minister read my inadequate words.

I am often asked about the impact her death has had on me. I have never been the same.

Up until her death, I had enjoyed a career full of successes and failures, but one always involved with building something or inventing a new way to do something – particularly in the world of electronic bond trading. I had built and managed five successful bond trading desks from scratch – Gordon Capital (the most successful zero-coupon trading desk ever), CIBC (a global bond trading desk), Dean Witter Canada, and my most successful one at First Marathon which lasted twelve years. My last trading desk (and the least successful) was at First Associates/Blackmont Capital. I was working there when Caroline died.

Her death took the wind out of my sails. I was sixty-one when she died and I had lots of time to do exciting things, but I had lost my drive and desire. I had written and published my book about the bond market – *In Your Best Interest* – complete with a great launch party at Jump in 2006. It was a proud moment for me, attended by one hundred of Bay Street's best with my daughters front and centre.

After she died, I was lost, to be blunt about it. Coming to my rescue were two great friends. After I was let go by Blackmont, I was adrift. I thought that I could become an Investment Advisor with my knowledge, personality, and media presence, but my heart was not in it. Both Bank of Montreal and RBC offered me employment as an Investment Advisor. I turned them down. One day, Debi Hewson, the CFO (now the CEO) of Odlum Brown, called and suggested that I consider going to work for them. I agreed to join them. We had forged a strong friendship going back to 1989-90 and had kept in touch. Initially, I thought that I could build a book of business based on my knowledge and the acclaim I received from my appearances on BNN. I did begin to attract clients, but I soon realized that it was not for me – particularly the compliance requirements. Debi had provided me with excellent support but I was happier in my role as a strategist for our sales force. This was, and is, a low-stress role and I have given it my best shot. It suited me because I was my own boss. I was unstressed. I had no management, personnel, or trading responsibilities.

Debi has a generous heart and she supported me and my charitable foundation generously, even opening the TSX with us one year. On another occasion, she attended an Oscar Party fundraiser.

Also coming to my rescue was Jeremy Fleming, a long-time trading colleague and friend. He took me to lunch one day in 2010 and observed that I looked lost. He was right. He introduced the subject of Freemasonry to me and I looked into it. In short, I became a Master Mason in the Harcourt lodge which was made up mostly of Bay Street people. I have enjoyed the support and friendships of my Masonic Brothers ever since. Masons support one another; they have let me speak on several occasions about my foundation.

Jeremy was a constant ally in my fundraising efforts and two other Brothers, Harrison Keenan and Scott Reid, became Directors of Care-Alive and made positive contributions.

My best friend, Stephen Reid, has been a constant positive factor in my life; seldom has a week gone by since 2007 that we have not talked or met each other for coffee or lunch. We met in 1984 in Oakville. Valerie had joined the Antoinettes Gymnastic Club as a competitive gymnast. At her first competition, I met Steve while we were taking down the equipment. Of course, this was a volunteer club run by the parents of the competitive stream. Steve said they were missing a treasurer, and being a serial volunteer, I took on the role. Together, we ran a club which prospered over the next ten years or so until our daughters ceased to compete. This club is in strong financial shape today, and we are proud of this. Our close relationship was further reinforced after he married Patricia Connor and they moved close to me in Hastings. I am fortunate that they live so close.

I finished the second and third editions of my book by 2011 but have had zero interest in updating it since then. I continued to appear on BNN (Business News Network) for several years, which resulted in copious publicity for Odlum Brown. The appearances gradually petered out and I made no attempt to revive them. This space has left me living a quiet, unstressed life in the small town of Hastings.

Impact on Kathleen

Caroline was extremely close to her mother. While I did my best to be a great father, it was Kathleen who was closer to CC. Here is what she wrote to Caroline on her thirty-second birthday:

DAUGHTER
What am I wishing you?
Strength for the future,
The feeling of seeing
A prized dream come true, a bright, carefree spirit,
But also the wisdom to know in your heart what is most right for you.
And always, I'm hoping that you will remember the most important thing by far:
How much you are loved, how proud I am, always, and how wonderfully special you are.
Happy birthday, love you lots, Momma, xox

Kathleen's Reflections on the Night the Police Arrived at the Door

It was Easter Sunday and Valerie and Caroline had been here with me for the weekend. We had a great time celebrating CC's birthday, and then the girls left for Toronto in high spirits.

It was after midnight and we had not yet fallen asleep when there was a banging on the front door. We wondered who it could possibly be at that hour. Bill went to the door and opened it to two policemen. They asked to speak to me. We both immediately thought there had been a car accident. The police told me that Caroline had been found dead at her apartment earlier that evening. I can't remember anything else they said, and I didn't write anything in my journal for three weeks, so the following is what I learned from Tannis and Valerie when they arrived here around 2 a.m.

Sunday, April 29, 2007 **(Kathleen's journal)**

Caroline has been dead three weeks. I am feeling especially sad today because it is finally hitting me that she is not coming back. She will not call up with a "Hiya momsy." The most recent gift she gave me – a pink visor and flamingo socks from Las Vegas – is the last gift – ever! She is here in the urn but she is not able to speak to me. I will not hear her happy voice, and I only have pictures to remind me of her smile.

For the past three weeks I have kept busy – first planning the service and then the actual day – not wanting it to ever end – not wanting to say goodbye – not wanting to face the inevitable.

Since then I have seen Tannis twice and stayed overnight in Caroline's bed both times. We have been sorting through Caroline's things.

Had a long conversation with Hope (cousin) yesterday. She lost a baby (only four days old) some long time ago but still feels the need to talk about it. Linda (Bill's sister) also called that evening. She too lost a baby at six weeks.

Reflections on the previous paragraph – interesting how people open up to others when they feel that there will be an understanding – and telling, that even after many years they still want to share their loss. Another woman who lives at the end of our lake came to see me and tell me about her daughter who was killed in a car accident at twenty-one on her way to her first job after graduating in nursing. She lent me several books that had been helpful for her.

Thursday, May 17, 2007 **(Kathleen's journal)**

Just got home from four nights away and a sense of lethargy took over me. It was raining and I was all alone. Caroline had bought tickets to OKLAHOMA at Stratford for my birthday/Mother's Day for me to go with Valerie and her. Instead, Valerie and I invited Tannis to accompany us. It was a bittersweet day but we managed to get through it.

Monday I spent sorting through Caroline's things at the apartment. In the evening I picked up Valerie to go and watch her and Tannis play in the first soccer game of the outdoor season. Their team is called "CC Cosmos" in honour of Caroline, who was the impetus behind getting the team together!

June 24, 2007 **(Kathleen's journal)**

Again, today I am very sad. Thinking about the upcoming weekend with the family and, knowing Caroline won't be a part of it, just makes me want to cry and I have cried a lot this morning.

Today is my parents' wedding anniversary so I am thinking of them too, and wondering if they can feel what's happening here at the moment. I mean, I don't really believe in an afterlife, but I so wish I had them to talk to and cry with.

July 27, 2007 **(Kathleen's journal)**

My last day at Caroline's apartment. I am so sad to think that this is the last time I will sleep in her room and feel the comfort of knowing she had been here. Even though most of the furniture is now gone, it is still her room. In this apartment she and Tannis spent many happy times, had many parties, and shared many thoughts. It seems that this is another "final" to the finals I have already passed through.

I had breakfast with Valerie yesterday. She is still wrestling with Caroline actually being gone. She doesn't want to acknowledge the depth of despair that one must, when one accepts the death of a loved one. Perhaps her time in France with Hank will help. I hope so.

(I took pictures of her room, the door to the apartment with the number 706, and the outside of the building showing 606 Avenue Road.)

Kathleen:

I am very lucky that I had the last day with Caroline. She and Valerie were here to celebrate Easter and her birthday, which was April 4. We hugged and kissed and told each other how much we loved each other – so no regrets. And I say to everyone – tell the treasured people in your life how much you love them every chance you get.

Impact on Tannis

Tannis Kynoch and Caroline became roommates, mostly as a result of their mutual love for movies and TIFF. They had many friends in common.

It was Tannis who discovered Caroline slumped on their apartment floor and not breathing. It was too late for the EMS people to revive her. I have never spoken with her about it since. I can barely imagine the traumatic impact on her.

Tannis became a stalwart member of our foundation, contributing mightily to our fundraising initiatives – particularly our Oscar-themed parties and the Bay Street Slo-Pitch tournament. She got us this latter event because of her connections.

She also did the due diligence which led to our becoming a significant contributor to the Lions Foundation's seizure response program. Ultimately, we sponsored twenty-seven such dogs.

Impact on Kirsty Robertson

CC's great friend (yes, another great friend), Kirsty Robertson, a fellow undergrad at Bishop's, penned the following which appeared in *The Globe and Mail* in memoriam of Caroline in 2009.

Not a minute, hour or day goes by that we, the family, friends and colleagues of Caroline, do not think of her or remember her. I remember Caroline leaning on a friend, any friend would do, her arm in the "Caroline hug," hand hooked behind the neck and around a shoulder. She always had an excellent grip in her hugs – they made you feel like you were the most important person on Earth. But this was par for the course, for Caroline excelled at taking a mundane moment and making it special, her spirit was irrepressible and extraordinary, and she was the queen of the brilliantly hilarious non-sequitur: "Spartacus gives me tingles," she once announced, apropos of nothing. We had a wall in our apartment in Lennoxville covered in such sayings – a compendium of the workings of Caroline's beautiful mind, cut shockingly and unexpectedly short on April 8, 2007 when she passed away after an Easter weekend spent with her family, a time of happiness made complete with Caroline and her younger sister Val driving back to Toronto belting out show tunes (no doubt punctuated by Caroline's pointed finger in the air keeping the beat, and her favourite expression of the moment, "superstah!").

Bishop's colour might have been purple but Caroline painted that town red. There were very few clubs she did not join, not a lot she didn't do – from playing softball and numerous other intramurals, to singing in the choir, to being a member of CJMQ, Entertainment Editor of The Campus, an editor of the Bishop's Directory, an actor in Theatre Activ, a member of the Model UN – a sometimes active participant in the "I Will Never Eat Another Morsel of Poutine" club, and one of the Bakery Girls (the appellation given to a group of CJMQers living above what was then Green's Bakery, a spot that became a location so central that after a time bakery came to be an adjective and a compliment – (O yes, I know her, she's so bakery!). Although she never finished her degree, Caroline landed firmly on her feet after leaving Bishop's in 1999, travelling regularly and visiting Australia, Cuba, The United States, Europe, and Africa (collecting friends along the way), working on Bay Street, and participating annually in the Toronto Film Festival where her photographic memory for film credits and obscure film trivia served her well.

It took me a long time to describe the radiance of Caroline's personality and to try to convey the devastating impact of her loss. It always seemed that Caroline exceeded any capacity of language to describe her, that the words simply didn't exist. But perhaps they were there all along, where it began. If a lounge singer ever got it right, it was Neil Diamond. At her memorial service, hundreds of people hummed the opening bars of "Sweet Caroline," voices cracking in the verse, breaking into song in the famous chorus – BA BA BA – the words carrying out the front door of the funeral home and up above the streets to the sky. The world is a little darker without her, for she was bright as yellow, our C.C., our Caroleaner, Petal, Carolinus, Sweet Caroline.

THE JOURNEY BEGINS

CHAPTER 3

The Event

Subject: Urgent
"Call me anytime, day or night"

On the morning of April 9, 2007, I awoke to a blinking Blackberry. I was on a golf fling in Myrtle Beach with eleven buddies from Scarboro Golf Club. It was Easter weekend. Most nights, we would all go out to a steak house, piano bar, or other restaurant. In the early evening of April 8, the guys were getting ready to go out.

However, I was feeling out of sorts and nauseous in a very odd and unsettled way. I decided to not go out.

That Blackberry message the next morning would haunt me forever. The message was from my daughter Valerie asking me to please call her as soon as I picked up the message. I called immediately.

"It's Caroline. She died!"

Later, I calculated that I began feeling nauseous the night before at the same time as Caroline was dying.

I was numb.

Valerie and Caroline had spent Easter weekend with their mother, Kathleen, in the country. They had a wonderful time, singing and dancing. When Valerie dropped

Caroline off at her apartment on Avenue Road in Toronto, Valerie asked if she wanted to watch a movie together. Caroline begged off and went into her apartment alone. Caroline's roommate, Tannis was not home. Apparently, Caroline had a seizure while sitting on the couch and slid to the floor unconscious. Tannis found her and immediately called EMS, but it was too late. They could not revive her. Later, we learned she died from SUDEP (*Sudden Unexpected Death in Epilepsy*). At the time, we had never heard of it. Tannis called Valerie immediately and Valerie sped to reach her mother before the police did. Valerie did not have my travel coordinates so the sheriff in Myrtle Beach did not know where I was. Valerie had to resort to a Blackberry message.

The rest of the day I was wracked with a shaking sobbing, the likes of which I had never experienced. I had to remove my contact lenses as my eyes were so swollen from crying.

Word spread quickly. A former girlfriend, Kim Stephany, called and volunteered to fly down and come home with me. I welcomed her offer but I was in no condition to accept. I was having difficulty functioning with my own arrangements but it would have been wonderful to have someone with me. It was a genuine and wonderful offer.

What followed was one, long, horrifying blur. I could not imagine life without Caroline. Tears fell uncontrollably. I had to inform my golf friends and then I headed for home. I was numb and not thinking straight. It took me a while to figure out how to get home. Eventually I went for a long walk on the beach trying to understand the meaning of it all and then I had to scramble to get home. Some friends called me to console me. It was an extremely arduous day and my recollection is mostly one of crying hard in airport lounges and on the plane and then running into the arms of Valerie and Kathleen.

Valerie and I headed for my condo while Kathleen stayed with Tannis.

Kathleen:

Tannis had gotten home to find Caroline slumped on the floor beside the couch. She discovered she was not breathing. She called 911. She performed CPR to no avail. We have not discussed this since. I often wanted to, but I felt that Tannis had been traumatized by the experience and so I avoided the subject.

For whatever reason, Tannis was not allowed to stay in the apartment that night. Just as well, as she probably had no desire to. She went with the police to Valerie's apartment and woke her up. Valerie will best be able to fill in what happened after that. When they arrived here we talked and talked but I can't remember details. I don't even remember when we went to the airport to meet Hank

Email: *Tuesday, April 3, 2007. 6:23:34 pm*
From: Caroline Cunningham
To: Hank Cunningham
We could do lunch tomorrow?

Tomorrow happened to be her thirty-second birthday and so we met at Reds Restaurant on Adelaide Street and had a wonderful lunch. She even enjoyed a rare glass of wine (at lunch that is!). She arrived in high spirits, had just had her hair done, and said she was looking forward to the Easter weekend with Valerie and their mother at Stoney Lake. I was heading for a weekend of golf with eleven pals from Scarboro Golf Club on our annual jaunt. That year, it coincided with Easter weekend. Thus, I'd celebrated Easter at my home in Hastings the previous weekend when we had our normal raucous time and I captured my last photos of Caroline as she and Valerie danced in front of the fireplace. They were dancing to "Proud Mary" by John Fogerty and, as they often did, doing the "Dad dance!"

We parted after lunch with hugs and kisses. It was the last time I saw her alive.

She died four days later. For years, I came back to Reds and sat at that same spot at the bar on the anniversary of her birthday.

Last Photo of Caroline

Chapter 4

The Service

From: Jeremy Fleming (close friend)

"It was a beautiful service. I remember someone told me once that the true measure of a man is not so much how he handles things when they are going well, but rather how he deals with events when they are not going so well. You did her proud."

The shock permeated us but we knew that we had to organize a service to honour her. We quickly chose the Humphrey Miles Funeral home on Bayview Avenue in Toronto. Kathleen contacted a Unitarian Minister, Doreen Peever, from St. Catharines, who had performed the services for her parents. We booked her and the funeral home for Saturday, April 14th.

Since then, we have walked this incredibly lonely and unique path that grieving people walk. I have experienced, and continue to experience, the various stages of grief: **anger, disbelief, sadness, and acceptance**.

Caroline was cremated on Wednesday, April 11. Myself and Valerie, Tannis and her sister Lynn, and Kathleen and Bill all went to the crematorium to say our final goodbyes.

When it was over, it sunk in that she really was dead and not coming back.

At the service, Valerie and Tannis spoke bravely and beautifully. Their eulogies are included in Chapters 1 and 2, respectively.

The funeral home put together a video with music which played for the hour before the service started. Kathleen chose wonderful music. The music playing as the pictures flashed on the screen included "Feels Like Home" by Chantal Kreviazuk (this song still brings tears to my eyes), "Songbird" by Eva Cassidy, and "You've Got a Friend" by Carole King. "Songbird" was written by Christine McVie of Fleetwood Mac, and recorded by them, but the Eva Cassidy version is much more haunting. The prelude to the service was "Angel" by Sarah McLaughlin, and the reflective song after the eulogy was "She's Got a Way" by Billy Joel.

Doreen Peever, chaplain of the Unitarian Congregation in St. Catharines, conducted the service. The service went well considering. Although it was very sad it ended on an up note - as we had hoped. The last song was, of course, CC's favourite: "Sweet Caroline" by Neil Diamond. She always had it played at the end of an evening of dancing. When it played, our row, Kathleen, Tannis, Valerie, and me, began to sway with the music and everyone present joined in.

To this day, I have little to no memory of those friends and family of mine who attended. Once in a while, I review the guest book to remind myself of all the wonderful people who attended. Of course, we received a tsunami of condolences, cards, and emails.

I was unable to speak. It was just too much for me. No matter how many speeches I have given or how many television appearances I have made, I could not have uttered more than a few words before breaking down.

Tannis and Valerie delivered brilliant eulogies; they both were very brave. After reading them, you know everything you need to know about Caroline.

The funeral home was jammed to overflow condition with at least five hundred people present. I don't think they could have squeezed in another person. The service started twenty minutes late as people were still arriving. People were lining the hallways and filling the lobby. The enormous volume of online tributes illustrates how many people Caroline touched. A couple even came from Holland - Ervin and Martine. They are cousins of her friend Teresa van der Post. Caroline went on the safari with them. Several other Dutch people sent their condolences. My Cunningham relatives came from across the country - from Newfoundland to Edmonton.

Our friends, the Holroydes from Winnipeg, came also.

Kathleen: One of my friends from Montreal also came with her husband. There were many Sweet Adelines at the service and, to my surprise, many people from my old workplace.

Caroline's friends showed up en masse. Five of her still close friends from school days put together a beautiful album of remembrance containing photos, poetry, and their thoughts. It makes me cry every time I read through it. They said everything so beautifully. Two of her friends, Lindsay and Evita, were pregnant. I remember my grandmother talking about when one life is snuffed out, another baby is born, thereby continuing the cycle of life.

From: **Kevin Sullivan (CEO, GMP Capital)**

Hank, on behalf of myself and everyone at GMP, I wanted to pass on our sincere condolences for your loss. Caroline was a very big part of the fabric of GMP and had many admirers and dear friends. Her positive attitude and smiling face will be sorely missed and never forgotten. Our entire firm is in a state of shock and we know our loss pales in comparison to yours and your family. If there is absolutely anything GMP or I can do during this difficult period by all means just ask. We genuinely feel the need to contribute as a way to deal with our own grief. It is most unfortunate that I personally will not be able to attend Saturday's memorial. I have long-established travel plans that cannot be changed. I will however be giving a tribute to Caroline at our AGM on April 18th at 10:00 a.m. in the TSX auditorium. If you are feeling up to it, we would be very pleased if you and your family can attend.

Much strength to you during this difficult time.
Kevin

GMP (Caroline worked there for seven-and-a-half years and was loved by all) came through with more than flying colours for us and Caroline. I had worked with most of the key GMP personnel at First Marathon for ten years or so; thus, we were close. With Caroline working there, it became a family atmosphere when I visited them.

After the service, GMP arranged for, and paid the total cost of, a memorial party at Vertical Restaurant. I am not sure who the principals were who stepped up to the plate, but certainly JoAnne Stansfield was a major factor as was Kevin Sullivan, the CEO. GMP also arranged limos for anyone who needed one (including driving the chaplain back and forth from St. Catharines). The limo company people simply loved Caroline. She had booked all the limos for the executives and for herself. She did so in Caroline-fashion, by getting to know them and by treating them well. When they spoke to her, it was as if they were the most important people. She always did this with a bubbly, lively approach.

There were some fine speeches from JoAnne Stansfield and the evening carried on. Nicolle Weir, a close friend of CC's, donated three hundred fir saplings for people to plant in her memory.

At the end of the evening, with a glass of champagne in my hand, I was with Valerie and Jamie Price, a friend who was very close to Caroline and Valerie. He was also one of my traders. We lingered and did not want the moment to end. There was some reminiscence about the One Drink Club, founded by Valerie, Jamie, Caroline, and another great friend, Nataly Alves, also one of my traders. They would seek out the bar with the cheapest drinks and appetizers!!! Movenpick was the best!

Again, the evening was a giant blur and I do not know how many people were there.

Of course, there was Caroline's company, GMP. All who worked with her there loved her as much as we did. It was amazing. At the reception, they also had a running collage of photos. I stayed late as I didn't want the day to end. I didn't want to face reality yet. I needed to grieve. I will come out of the dark, I know, because I want to go on in happiness.

Chapter 5

The Journey

From Scott Cunningham (Hank's brother)
Dear Kathleen, Hank, Valerie:

The stars over Waterloo seemed extra bright last night. I was looking for the answer to why, why, why.

I picked one that seemed to be the brightest and this star will always remind me of Caroline.

A zest for life, her full speed ahead attitude will never be forgotten, hopefully the "why" will fade.

Hank, I have always looked up to you in life: you are a mentor to me. If I could trade places, if I could ease the pain, I would not hesitate.

From Nadya, Marina, and myself, our thoughts are only of you and your family.

The grieving period began. Much has been written about grief. Much of it meant little to me. It is an entirely personal event and thus cannot be truly shared with anyone else. How the death of someone so beloved affects those closest to her varies from person to person. I have discussed her impact on us in Chapter 2.

I have not come across a single book about grief that resonated with me. Several poems did; Valerie included the e. e. cummings poem in her eulogy.

I came across an author, Mary Rykov, who wrote the following after the death of her father:

Grief is unique and personal and it can be collective. Ubiquitous and inclusive: nobody lives a life devoid of grief. For the gift of love, we must suffer the debt of loss in gratitude for having loved and been loved. Nothing can assuage this pain. Rather, we must take time and space to live grief fully, honouring it to ourselves and – as best we can –comforting others as they grieve. We have no choice because the pain we neglect or stifle only festers and grows stronger.

The intensity of grief ebbs and flows like a tide that dims with the distance of time but never disappears entirely. Grief spirals back, returning to bite again, sometimes unexpectedly and with shocking intensity. But our death-defying, youth-worshipping culture provides no models for dealing with emotional pain. Instead of attending to pain and learning – exploring, listening – we instead deny sadness. Or we medicalize it.

This sums up my feelings on grief almost perfectly.

I was an Executive Vice President at Blackmont Capital and managed their bond trading desk. Two of Caroline's (and Valerie's) best friends, Nataly Bozzo and Jamie Price, were my traders. I could not go back at first. Even when I did return, a couple of weeks later, it was still too soon. The wounds were raw.

Reality set in. After the service and party, we were left to deal with our grief alone. We had the unenviable, and at least to me, gruesome, task of dealing with all her things in her apartment. I remember bags of clothes going to Goodwill. We sifted through her large collection of books, CDs, and dishes with some us taking a few items for keepsakes. Caroline had been making more money than she could spend and that is saying a lot! She wanted to purchase a high-quality entertainment system, complete with a top-end television and surround sound. She asked me to go to Best Buy with her for moral support and to assist in the negotiations. In typical Caroline fashion, she struck the right chord with the sales person. When she found the unit which she favoured, she came to me for negotiating help. She shuttled back and forth a few times and finally closed her deal.

At the apartment, no one knew what to do with this stereo unit so I claimed it and installed it in my condo.

We were emotionally spent after this ordeal. Valerie and I decided to take a break and spent five days at a resort in Freeport, Bahamas. This was good tonic for us. I taught her how to play blackjack; we cleaned up at the casino and spent all our winnings in Caroline fashion, including swimming in the ocean with dolphins.

We needed that break. We were to take two more vacations which I will describe later.

Parents are not supposed to outlive their children. It is the wrong order of things. In the mammalian world, parents grieve as heavily as do humans, sometimes withering and dying after losing a child. A dramatic example of this type of grieving occurred in 2018 when a female orca lost her calf not long after birth and, for eighteen days, she pushed her dead calf to the surface in a vain attempt to revive it.[1] Elephants are known to weep when they lose a calf and they also visit the remains of their children.

In the human world, when parents lose a child, disbelief sets in immediately and it becomes difficult to maintain existing relationships. Because Care-Alive, our charitable foundation, became well known in the epilepsy community, I met several people who had lost children to SUDEP. In one case, a woman's daughter had not had a seizure in nine years but then she died in her sleep at age twenty-one. This woman's family went to pieces. Divorce followed plus lots of recrimination and a descent into drugs and alcohol.

While the shock was still new and the wounds fresh, we did not fall apart. It is a very lonely road that we walk, those of us who have lost a child. The best that we can do is commiserate with our fellow voyagers on this path because they are the only ones who understand. We can also offer our experiences to those who have lost a child or loved one more recently than we have. I have bonded with many such people who knew what I had experienced and I was able to console them also. Consoling them meant mostly listening and sharing how I was coping. I would discuss the two principal themes of anger and denial; this helped. Also, I encouraged seeking counselling to at least have someone to talk to. I encouraged them to keep in touch with me as well.

Speaking of counselling, I discovered how quirkily the mind can work. Not long ago, I told Valerie how I had got through our early days without needing to see anyone.

1 https://www.cnn.com/2018/08/12/us/orca-whale-not-carrying-dead-baby-trnd/index.html

She reminded me that I had sought and met a counsellor on at least three occasions! I remember meeting a lovely woman in Rosedale and we talked a lot about France!

It is impossible to explain without emotions taking over. We were still angry and in denial. Two lessons began to emerge:

1. The pain and anger begin to ebb slowly, and
2. The acceptance level rises. It sinks in that she is not coming back.

It took me **ten** years to finally declare myself mostly healed. While that is a huge positive, I find that emotions still run strong and are at all times near the surface. I think of her constantly.

What Not to Say and What to Say

There should be courses to educate well-meaning individuals in what to say and not to say to those who are grieving. In fact, there are courses; one is entitled "Death and Dying." It focuses on teaching how to cope with grief and bereavement.

The advice offered to us, while well-meaning, often hurt.

Here are examples of phrases which should never be used:

1. "She is in a better place now!!!" What is wrong with some people? Of course she is not in a better place!
2. Any phrase beginning with *at least:* "At least you have another child." This was all too common.
3. "Let me know if you need anything."
4. "Stay strong" or "Be strong."

On the other hand, there are things you should say and do:

1. "I am so sorry" is fine.

Here are some others:

2. "Whatever you are feeling, and whenever you are feeling it, it's OK."

3. "I know how much you loved her."
4. "I wish I had the right words for you."
5. "I can't imagine what you are going through, but I am here to listen if you need me."

Better yet, and this is my preferred approach to someone grieving, is to do something practical and launch into action. Bring food, listen, reach out during holidays. Just do something without being asked.[1, 2]

Don't offer; just do it. Drop in and do laundry, take care of the kids for a few hours, and talk about the person who died. Tell some unheard stories or anecdotes about them. Volunteer for a cause.

At my farm in Hastings, I left her room unchanged. I had given her and Valerie a budget to decorate their rooms and, naturally, Caroline went retro with antiques! Her room became a museum with her golf clubs, tennis racquet, a boomerang from her Australian adventure, plus her favourite blanket from her African vacation. It stayed that way until recently, but more on that later. When visitors slept in her bed, they felt her presence all around them. Her presence is magnified at Thanksgiving, Christmas, and Easter. We took some photos of an image behind my house which resembled her. Valerie, Vincent and I all saw it. It was eerie. It was a blue image that moved around and resembled Caroline. We could not explain it. We only saw it the one time.

Later, when we embarked on our charitable work, she would come to me at different times and say: "Keep up the good work, Dad."

Caroline loved butterflies. Once, when Valerie was presenting the Caroline Cunningham trophy at the Bay Street Stampede, a Monarch butterfly approached Valerie and hung around for several minutes, landing on her shoulder and resting there. I am not sure of the sightings or experiences of the others, but enough of these things have happened to me to raise my belief in the paranormal.

---

1 https://www.realsimple.com/work-life/grief-what-not-to-say

2 https://www.nytimes.com/2019/02/14/smarter-living/what-to-say-and-what-not-to-say-to-someone-whos-grieving.html

Valerie had never been to Europe, so I planned a trip to France where we would spend a few days in Paris and then take the TGV south to Provence and Nice. In Paris, we stayed at my favourite hotel, Le Duc du St. Simon, in the 7th District. The hotel picked us up at Charles de Gaulle; our rooms were not ready so we had café crème, croissants, and jam in the white cobblestone courtyard. For years, I had told my daughters how great the coffee was and how fresh the food was in France. She had some coffee and a bite of a croissant, looked at me, and said: "I get it, Dad!"

The wonderful food in France was certainly a comfort to us and a distraction. We would dine at a café and immerse ourselves in the passersby, emptying ourselves of our thoughts and emotions as we attempted to analyze their lives. This was therapeutic. We became emotional mostly at dinnertime, reminiscing about our times with Caroline and also shedding tears for a holiday CC would never experience.

We spent a few nights in Paris and took in the Lido among other things. The French mistook Valerie for my mistress!

We took the TGV to Avignon, where we stayed for five days at L'Europe, the hotel where Napoleon once stayed. We toured Van Gogh territory and visited wineries in Gigondas and Chateau Neuf de Pape. Mostly, Valerie fell in love with Avignon itself in a mystical way, no doubt part of the grieving and healing process. Avignon proved to be a magical place for Valerie as she found a particular park overlooking the Rhone where she became lost in herself.

We were so numb still that we would hang out at cafés, indulging in people-watching. Doing so helped us to empty our minds of grief. We also consumed reasonable quantities of wine, champagne, and wonderful food. Café crème became a staple for breakfast!

Then it was back on the TGV for the long and wonderful trip back to Paris. We stayed at the same hotel. Valerie suggested we get our boarding passes the night before. We logged in and, lo and behold, Air Canada offered us a complimentary upgrade to first class! We hit the yes button in record time and enjoyed a wonderful trip home.

I have been asked what kind of discussions we had during our time together on this vacation. We had many emotional times, most frequently at dinner. While some of them were raw, teary moments, some of them were positive as we remembered a lot of the good and great times we enjoyed with Caroline. For her part, Valerie said she could not carry on with her job and career and would look to become a bartender, which would occupy her but not require much in the way of intellectual effort.

It made me sad on more than one occasion when it struck me that Valerie and I were on a vacation, the likes of which CC would never get to enjoy.

My memories of Nice are mostly of Valerie just floating endlessly in the Mediterranean.

On the TGV back to Paris, I came to some conclusions about myself and my life. I made up my mind to clear my personal and professional slate and make significant changes.

After this vacation, we booked separate ones. Valerie proceeded on the kind of adventure her sister would have planned: a trip to the Galapagos Islands with a group of young people sponsored by the GAP Adventure Company. Valerie had discussed taking such a vacation with Caroline, who had urged her to go and pay for it later as she often did. Thus, Valerie finally went to the Galapagos Islands. Caroline did not know that Valerie finally took this trip.

For my part, I opted to go on my first cruise ever: up the B.C. coast to Alaska. I took wonderful photos and enjoyed the experience.

Again, these vacations may have been more in her honour than anything else. Our grief was too raw to discuss with anyone, so our thoughts remained with ourselves.

Dear Valerie,

I am writing this in my beloved gazebo, having just had a wonderful rib steak, and I have a glass of Clos de Vougeot Grand Cru 2005 in my hand.

As you know, these "hallmark" days have never been a big deal for me; nevertheless, I am using this one, Father's Day, for reflection about my children.

I am the proudest father in the world. While being an imperfect man, replete with all manner of flaws and one who has made lots of mistakes, co-producing my children has been my greatest achievement. Nothing else I have done comes even close. I have said to you both, as a father, I tried to become your hero and role model. I did my best and I would like to think that I succeeded, at least partly.

While I poured myself into your and Caroline's life while you were growing up, I always believed that one raises one's children to leave the nest and join the adult world. I will never be a clingy dad, but I would obviously like to keep in close touch.

You are building your own life now, with Vincent, your own set of friends, your career, and your ambitions, dreams, and hopes of adventures. I was/am never so proud as when someone complimented me on the maturity and presence of my daughters and what beautiful people they were. We raised you this way because we thought it was the right thing to do.

Caroline's life ended far too soon and this has changed me forever. It is the wrong order of things.

However, I still have one star shining brightly: you.

I am so proud of the person you have become and are still becoming. You combine so many wonderful traits: intelligence, charisma, interpersonal skills, athleticism, drive, and dynamism to name a few. I remain the proudest dad in the world.

All my love,
Dad
xoxoxoxoxoxo

April 8, 2015

It has been eight years now. On this anniversary, I am in Hastings. It is a cool, windy, overcast day with steel-grey clouds. Nasty weather is forecast, possibly including freezing rain.

I do not feel like doing anything this year. I am wearing a Care-Alive hoodie and drinking water from one of the souvenir mugs from Valerie's wedding. All I plan to do today is go for a long walk and spend some time in my small hardwood forest where I meditate. I have not done that for a while. I began to feel her presence yesterday and she is all around me. No doubt she will visit me in the forest.

Of course, when I visited my forest later in the day and meditated for thirty minutes or so she did come to me; and, once again, as she flew past me, she told me: "I am OK, Pops!"

I have had many extrasensory moments: many déjà vu experiences, or feelings that I have been somewhere before or was someone else. My feelings of extreme queasiness during the moments when she was dying were no coincidence. I was feeling her pain. We have had many ESP moments; seeing her blonde hair in a crowd, hearing her voice, seeing visions. Other times when she comes to me, she says: "Keep up the good work!" I slept in her bed that night and felt her spirit all around me.

I had thought of taking the train to Montreal or going to New York. In the end, I just decided to go nowhere and lie low.

Eight years and this is still very painful. I am numb and feel queasy enough to be ill.

As always, I am anxious to put this day behind me. My life becomes suspended in early April with her birthday and passing being just four days apart. It is a "heavy" day for sure, an understatement if there ever was one. I thought that perhaps the pain would be less this year but it is taking a big toll. I am not sure if I can watch the service again, but perhaps I need a big cry.

April 8, 2017

For the tenth anniversary of Caroline's passing, Valerie thought that it would be a good opportunity to throw a "party" to mark this milestone. I agreed and thus we booked the Oak Room at the Cambridge Club (where I had been a long-term member) and invited family, friends, Eric Sinclair from the TMX, Jeremy Fleming, Dr. Donner and Ayala Beck from SickKids Hospital, and fifty others.

It turned out to be a huge success. There were lots of children, including, of course, the irrepressible and delightful Charlie (my granddaughter), who made friends with everyone.

There were no speeches. It was a gathering to remember and honour her, and it had a cathartic effect on me. Afterwards, a few days later, I declared myself healed and hence, I thought about possibly writing a book. Of course, emotions continue to run high but I have so much more life to me now. This was a day of passage for me. I am not sure how it affected others.

Since that day, I can speak about her and our experiences more openly than at any time over the first ten years. I truly am healed.

April 8, 2018

What a difference a year makes. This day marked the eleventh anniversary of her passing. As I mentioned above, I felt myself healed and feeling well enough to begin writing this book. I could not have even contemplated doing so just one year ago. Unlike past years, I do not feel queasy and ill. The dread is gone. She comes to me, of course, and I feel her all around me, but I am more at peace. I drove into Toronto to have brunch with Valerie, Kathleen, and Bill. Charlie was having breakfast with Vincent but they joined us later. Vincent went home and the rest of us drove to CC's tree in Trinity-Bellwoods Park. It was a nasty, windy day, near zero, so we did not linger long. Underscoring how much Charlie has added to our lives, she engaged in a game of hide-and-seek with Valerie around the trunk of the tree.

She is such a delight.

Charlie

I drove home in time to watch the finale of the Masters Golf Tournament. Of course, this could not do anything but remind me of that Easter weekend eleven years ago when I was on a golf trip. I have barely touched a golf club since and if I do, I do not keep score. In fact, I finally gave away my golf clubs to Vincent.

I am feeling the best that I have in these past eleven years and, as I have mentioned, I feel healed at the levels of acceptance and anger. Emotions, however, are always near the surface. Unlike other years, I am not overcome with grief. I feel her presence but I am calm. It was wonderful to see Valerie and CC's friends posting so many wonderful photos on April 4, her birthday. Today is a sombre day; perhaps some of her friends will meet us at her tree.

March 23, 2019

Spring is arriving, albeit haltingly. It does bring April with it and, as in the previous eleven years, the fourth and eighth of April loom over me and my family.

I have been dreaming a lot about Caroline lately; no particular theme, but she is in my mind, surrounded by her great friends, as always.

I will be in Toronto on her birthday, April 4, and I am not sure what I will do or where I will be on April 8. On Purple Day, I am attending a gathering at Queen's Park. Several epilepsy associations will be there. The goal of this day, organized by Premier Ford's office, is to promote permanent funding. One of his advisors has connections with Epilepsy Toronto.

I will use this time to add further to my book.

April 4 has come and gone. Valerie and I enjoyed a wonderful meal at Canoe, preceded by a champagne cocktail, of course. Jeff, the award-winning mixologist, remembered us from all of our parties there and he certainly remembered Caroline. We ended up at Reds for a nightcap where we sat exactly where CC and I sat on her birthday, four days prior to her death.

It is Sunday, April 7; I have been having trouble sleeping lately. Tomorrow is almost here. I plan to do nothing except possibly meditate in my forest and take a long walk.

I am feeling the chills and her presence is growing around me. It is a gathering force which envelops me. Thus far, I feel better than in previous years, but I feel a period of gloominess approaching. I will just let it happen and embrace it, cry if I must, but, above all else, remember her.

April 8, 2019, 5:35 a.m.

It is rainy and overcast, as befits such a sad day. I still have the chills and I feel her spirit all around me as if she is trying to hug me. I have no plans today and will not likely leave my house except for a walk through my forest where I will undertake some meditation. No doubt she will come to me there.

As I felt last year, I am calm and nowhere near as despondent as in the earlier years. My attitude is more positive and I will spend a lot of time writing today.

Of course, Charlie makes a difference and she is now more aware than ever at six that her mom had a sister and she would have had an aunt. Such an empathetic child she is.

Grief

"*Grief fills the room up of my absent child.*" – King John, Act III, Scene IV,
William Shakespeare

Tributes

My Dear Hank,

I am glad you have her all around you. I planted her sapling today, and as I did, the sun came out. I wrapped it in burlap to protect it as if it were Caroline itself. She was your biggest fan and loved you with all her heart. What a special thing for a father to have; you were very special to her and to Val. This is a wonderful tribute to you; you are a great dad and friend.

All my love,
Joanne (Joanne Stansfield of GMP)

Part of our journey involved the tributes to her. As I have mentioned, she was well-loved at GMP in a family-type environment.

Then, there were the trees.

GMP was not done yet. The GMP people knew of CC's love for New York, where she may have moved eventually. Someone, and I will give JoAnne Stansfield the credit, researched and researched until they discovered the Central Park Conservancy. GMP's employees raised the required fifty thousand dollars out of their own pockets in no time for a tree dedicated to Caroline in Central Park, along with her name engraved on a red paving stone amidst those of many celebrities. We have visited it many times.

The Paving Stone

The Tree in Central Park

Regarding the Red Maple in Central Park - *Desiree Klein*

Desiree was yet another of Caroline's "great" friends. Great is not an overused adjective, as she cultivated friends of all types and genders from all corners of the world. Desiree was close enough to Caroline to do what the rest of us were unable to do: she frog-marched Caroline to the epilepsy clinic at Toronto Western Hospital. This hospital conducts the most advanced epilepsy research in Canada. Peter Carlin (an Honorary Board member of Care-Alive, our private foundation), runs a weekly clinic there. They performed a complete work-up on CC over two days. We have read the report. It was judged that she was not at risk!

Desiree, as it turned out, spent the summer of 2007 in New York and she worked closely with the Central Park people on the location of the tree as well as the type of tree. She also influenced the placement of the paving stone.

These are her words:

I liked the Red Maple because it is a "Canadian" tree (it stands on its own, independently from the other grouped trees around it, which reminds me of CC); it is near the Delacorte Theater (where Caroline would line up in the wee hours of the morning to watch free Shakespeare in the Park); and it is by the turtle pond, the Belvedere Castle, the MET museum, and across from the GREAT LAWN (where everyone hangs out on weekends - very cool/hip). It also sits in an area where children play. I felt that it represented all that Caroline was in life and loved in the Big Apple. Another nice thing about it is that it is a young tree so we can look forward to watching it grow and blossom and meet its full potential in the years ahead. Many of us have visited this famous tree and the paving stone.

I met the young woman from the Central Park Conservancy, Stephanie Donley, after Desiree had selected the tree and the red paving stone was in place. It was a Canadian Red maple, as mentioned, and Desiree had done a wonderful job selecting the location. We visited the tree first, and then Stephanie walked with me to the south end of Literary Walk where all the paving stones were laid out in the form of a compass. She showed me Caroline's stone: it took my breath away and I teared up immediately. I was not prepared to see such a permanent tribute to her. This was, and is, an enduring tribute to her, thanks to her generous colleagues at GMP. Her stone in in the north-west quadrant of the compass points to Canada. There are a lot of well-known names among these stones.

I recall having a picnic under the tree with Valerie and several of CC's friends, such as Evita, where we reminisced.

Valerie and Tannis at the tree

Valerie and CC's Friends

Valerie and I went on more than one occasion. One memorable visit was in December; I purchased tickets to see the famous Rockettes at Radio City Music Hall. A dazzling show! Of course, we visited the tree and stone. The Conservancy people had warned us not to decorate the tree as they would remove anything we placed on it. This did not deter us.

From time to time, various relatives and friends would ask us for directions and they were thus able to visit her tree and stone (see directions in Appendix A). One year, my niece Tarah (brother Scott's daughter), went to Central Park and had difficulty locating the tree. She informed Valerie who checked with the Central Park people. Unbeknownst to us, the tree had been damaged so badly after an ice storm that they replaced it. They neglected to inform us. Valerie learned this after talking with them. We were upset but resigned to this outcome. We accepted it as yet another moment of progress on our path. I have yet to see the replacement tree but it will not be the same thing.

The amazing generosity that went into planting the tree in the first place had done its job.

Stanley Park, Vancouver

There had been a violent windstorm in Vancouver in 2006 with peak winds of 114 miles per hour, which destroyed some ten thousand trees in Stanley Park, causing millions of dollars of damage. Caroline was well-loved by all of GMP's clients. One prominent Vancouver client, after hearing of the Central Park tree, decided to donate a tree in her name to replace one of the destroyed trees. For one thousand dollars, individuals could sponsor a tree planting anywhere in the Park. He donated ten thousand dollars to have a specific tree dedicated to her. Again, it was well chosen, in Ceperley Meadow, very near a children's playground. Along with Debi Hewson, CEO of Odlum Brown; good friend Barry Komar; and another friend Trina Richards; I dedicated her tree in the company of the Stanley Park official. As I work for Odlum Brown, a Vancouver-based firm, I have visited this tree many times; on every visit, I have struck up conversations with parents and grandparents playing near the tree. Some of them have asked me about the tree as they noticed me taking photographs.

Stanley Park, Vancouver

Barry Komar, Trina Richards, me, and Debra Hewson

Her tree, as can be seen in the photographs, is a young giant sequoia and it is growing beautifully.

Kathleen did her own research and discovered that the City of Toronto has a program to dedicate trees. She acted on this and there is now a beautiful young maple tree in Trinity-Bellwoods Park dedicated to CC. This made it easier for those who are unable to get to New York or Vancouver to pay their respects.

Another close friend of CC's was Nicolle Weir. She also worked at GMP and stayed close to Caroline through many important moments. She was also the coordinator for Valerie's wedding.

As mentioned earlier, at the party following the service, she donated three hundred fir saplings for people to plant in Caroline's honour. This was a generous act and these trees have flourished in many back yards. We get reports of people moving and transplanting their CC tree!

I planted a beautiful blue spruce outside her bedroom window in Hastings and it has matured beautifully. In the earlier years, I decorated it at Christmas, but now it is so tall that I need a stepladder to add the ornaments and lights!

In my view, this was another step on our path to recovery. All of these trees symbolize the love everyone had for Caroline and we all think of her when we see these trees.

For some time, I would call her direct line just to hear her voice as they left it as it was. They say that remembering a voice becomes difficult as time goes by. It was comforting for a while, at least, to hear her musical, bubbly greeting.

Caroline's chair remained empty for a long while with her sweater draped over it in the GMP trading room. Valerie and I were visiting JoAnne Stansfield one day and I sat in CC's chair and enjoyed being in it. Right there and then, JoAnne gave me CC's chair and I wheeled it home to my condo on Lombard Street. I use it every day in my country office.

To: Joanne Stansfield
Subject: Everything

Thank you from the bottom of my heart for all your magnificent gestures. I am using her chair right now. Let us know what to do with that beautiful but extremely large floral arrangement.

Affectionately,
Hank

Caroline's photo from GMP's Annual Report

At the time of GMP's Annual Meeting, they had included a full page on her in the Annual Report and we were present to hear CEO Kevin Sullivan's eloquent and emotional comments about our beloved Caroline.

In Memory of Caroline ("C.C.") Cunningham

Long-standing relationships - with both clients and colleagues - have always been at the core of GMP's culture. In 2007, GMP was saddened by the loss of a veteran team member and friend, Caroline ("C.C.") Cunningham.

Caroline joined GMP in December 2000 as a Sales Assistant on the institutional trading floor. She embodied the thriving and energetic GMP spirit through her willingness to lend a helping hand and aspiration to make our work environment an even better place. A strong believer in the importance of giving back to the community, Caroline was involved with many charitable organizations in Toronto.

On April 8, 2007, Caroline passed away suddenly. Her infectious smile, energy, and charm will always be remembered. Caroline was loved by everyone at GMP and is sadly missed. We are proud to continue Caroline's support of Right To Play, one of her favourite charitable causes.

GMP was in a hockey tournament and they dedicated their final game to CC, wearing black armbands with CC on them. Valerie and I attended and dropped the first puck, another giant emotional moment.

Chapter 6

Making a Difference

To help me in my journey on this troubled path, I adopted some of the principles of Buddhism. Chief among these is the idea of continuum... we live on through others.

It occurred to us that Caroline's continuum was to make a difference in the world of epilepsy, raising awareness of SUDEP, raising money for research, and helping the one in one hundred Canadians afflicted by it.

We decided to begin a foundation. I set the wheels in motion and called in a favour from a lawyer whose firm did a lot of charity applications. Our lawyer fast-tracked us, saving us about nine months, and thus, on January 1, 2009, The Caroline Cunningham Foundation for Epilepsy (CCFFE) came into being.

It was a long and unwieldy name. Joe Paonessa, married to one of Caroline's childhood friends, Nathalie, had the name "CareAlive" come to him when he was attending her funeral service. This is a play on words, sounding like her name but also calling attention to our principal goal of caring for those still alive. Joe attended one of our board meetings and, after he presented us with his proposed name, we adopted it instantly, going on to trademark the name and then using it on all our swag: T-shirts, water bottles, picnic hampers, and golf shirts, to name a few.

My Thoughts After Years One and Two

This seems to be an appropriate moment to write to you all, the Directors and Membersof *Care-Alive, the Caroline Cunningham Foundation for Epilepsy*, as we draw near to the end of our second year of existence. Admittedly, 2009 was a non-year for the most part, the highlight being the Oscar Party, something we all felt strongly about but would NEVER do again in that format. However, it did feel good and we will host more Oscar nights.

It is worth remembering that we are a private foundation and not a charity. I reiterate this because, while we are anxious to flesh out our organization, we are all volunteers and we cannot pay or receive salaries or have office overhead.

I offer my full gratitude for all the hard work and sacrifices you have all made. You have families, commitments, and full-time jobs, so hats off to you for your selfless dedication.

As a foundation, we can only advance funds to qualified donees such as charities, hospitals, schools, and, ugh, political parties! I appreciate that we all get stressed around our two main fundraisers. Stepping back for a moment, we might consider that that is all we should do per annum.

Mike Wekerle's generosity, one hundred thousand dollars, has given us a serious leg up and we can build on that. In my mind, we should be building our relationships with Yellow Bus, Freedom International, Odlum Brown, and others so that we have guaranteed sizeable donations annually. In addition, we should continue to "elephant hunt." I believe that we can function as an intermediary between those groups who are willing to donate to us and do not know exactly what to do with their money and those that have specific funding needs. That will be our role: to accept requests for funding and then decide which ones to allocate to.

We chose the private foundation route on purpose. Foundations are not charities, although, legally, they are charitable organizations with CRA authorization. While charities such as United Way maintain offices and personnel, chewing up at least thirty-five per cent of donations in the process, private foundations cannot pay salaries. Thus, we were, and are, volunteers. Our sole expenses were legal and accounting. Thus, ninety-nine per cent of donations given to us went towards the cause. Caroline would like that.

Besides myself as Chairman and CEO; the foundation included Valerie as President; Kathleen as Secretary (a tough, thankless job but she acquitted herself well); and my niece Rachelle McDonald (my brother Scott's daughter), as Treasurer. She did an outstanding job. Tannis was a Director and did the heavy lifting for our fundraising events.

In the early stages, we had big dreams and ideas. We met with the two top neurologists in Canada who treat adult epilepsy: Peter Carlin, head of research at Western Hospital, and Taufik Valiente, who, as a surgeon, operated on patients with extreme epilepsy. They both agreed to become honorary Directors of Care-Alive.

We thought that we could raise three or four million dollars and establish the first Chair for Epilepsy in Canada.

We also met with the key people at Toronto Hospital for Sick Children (SickKids). Caroline loved children. Dr. Elizabeth Donner, a wonderful person, was the head of the neurology department. While CC was treated as an adult, she loved children so much that it made sense for us to explore options with SickKids. If we had succeeded in establishing a Chair for Epilepsy in Canada, it would have been a joint effort with Toronto Western and SickKids. I had occasion to refer many people to SickKids and they were of particular help to these people. One of the sad elements of the world of epilepsy is the appalling lack of knowledge by doctors, nurses, and EMS people. Part of our mission (and indeed that of the top doctors and surgeons of the two hospitals) was the education of the neurological community. We helped to spread the word, along with other associations, and I would like to think that we moved the needle somewhat through educational pieces, countless interviews, plus our overall raising of awareness levels. One in a hundred people have epilepsy; that is over 350,000 Canadians, a large percentage of whom were and are woefully uninformed about this disorder.

When we wound down our foundation in 2018, we had donated one hundred thousand dollars to Toronto SickKids Hospital to create an endowment in Caroline's name. Her name will live on. The proceeds from this endowment will go to educating various individuals in the field of neurology. Donations to an endowment are eligible for charitable receipts so we have little doubt that this endowment will grow. Care-Alive would go on to make a distinguished name for itself in the world of epilepsy, raising awareness at an exponential rate.

This foundation accomplished two things:

First, it brought together Caroline's family: her father and mother and sister Valerie, her beloved cousin Rachelle McDonald, her roommate and close friend Tannis Kynoch, and other friends. Many of her friends opted not to join the foundation but were there every time we needed volunteers.

Second, it also helped us to focus on saving lives. We were able to do that and Caroline's name is now commemorated in two places:

First, *The Caroline Cunningham Youth Drop-in Centre* at the Epilepsy South Central Offices in Mississauga. This provides a medium for teens to get together and avoid the stigma of having epilepsy.

Second, a permanent endowment at Toronto SickKids Hospital. This endowment will produce funds to help educate those studying neurology and epilepsy.

At Epilepsy South Central Ontario

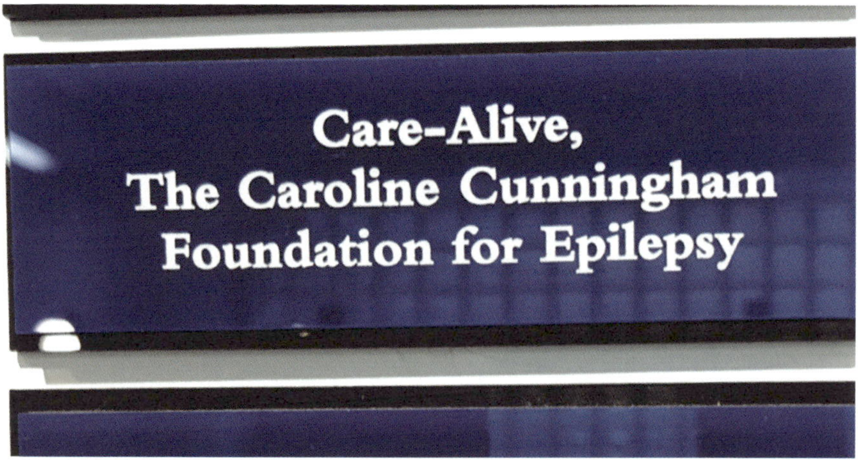

At Toronto SickKids Hospital

Besides that, as mentioned earlier, there are trees dedicated to her in Central Park, New York, Stanley Park in Vancouver, and Trinity Bellwods Park in Toronto. She will never be forgotten.

Our story is full of laughter, tears, and kindnesses. At the same time, it is overwhelmingly about grieving, healing, and our love for our precious Caroline.

We hoped that Care-Alive would make a difference in the world of epilepsy. We were stunned at the paucity of knowledge of this disorder. SUDEP was listed as the cause of death on the coroner's report.

What was that? (See Appendix B.)

We were to learn that, apart from the top neurological people, virtually no one, not regular neurologists (Caroline's own doctor was a case in point), nor GPs, nor EMS personnel, knew anything about epilepsy, never mind SUDEP. We determined to do something about it. In the end, we accomplished a lot. We raised over eight hundred thousand dollars and sponsored twenty-seven seizure response dogs. We sent kids to camp, we garnered publicity by opening the TSX on nine consecutive Purple Days, and **we saved lives**.

As anyone in the fundraising business knows, it is tough going as everyone with money is besieged on all sides by well-intentioned charities representing worthy causes.

Nevertheless, we embarked on our mission. First up was an Oscar Party. Caroline and Tannis were both heavy-duty film buffs and fixtures at the Toronto International Film Festival (TIFF). Thus, it seemed natural to hold an Oscar Party to raise funds. We quickly learned that you cannot charge too much for tickets. We ended up with a low-budget party, held in a party room at a condo. It might have been our most memorable party, but it was a lot of work!

Another year, we put on a black-tie TIFF gala at the Bell Lighthouse facility. It was a wonderful event and a great tribute to Caroline. We had the red carpet and a wonderful guest list, including one of the seizure dog recipients with her dog! The good news was that it was a genuine feel-good event. The less than good news was that, for all the effort us volunteers put in (again with Tannis spearheading the effort), we did not raise the amount of funds we needed.

It was not long after this that we decided to not host the Oscar Party again.

Next up was a baseball tournament where we were to be the designated charity for the day. We became the charity of record as a result of Tannis' friendship with the president of the Bay Street softball league. The previous charity had bowed out and so Tannis was able to have us added. This was a lot of work but we raised an adequate amount of funds. While Tannis did almost all the heavy lifting to run this tournament, there were scores of volunteers to do all manner of tasks (barbecuing, babysitting, face-painting, etc.). My chief role was to ensure the financial success of the tournament by calling on my Bay Street friends for donations. Peter Mcrae of Freedom Bond Brokers, Peter Conroy of Shorcan, and Debi Hewson, CEO of my own firm, Odlum Brown, were always generous; their support covered all the costs of the event. They supported our other fundraising events as well.

Care-Alive became quickly known in the epilepsy world for the awareness which we were raising and for caring for those still alive.

Caroline would like that.

By this time, recognizing that our giant goals and dreams were unattainable, we turned to the micro world of helping people. After due diligence, we elected to begin donating money to the Lions Foundation whose members train service dogs for visually impaired, hearing challenged, special needs, and autistic individuals. They also were beginning to raise seizure response dogs to be companions to those epilepsy sufferers needing constant care. We decided to help them grow this program. For every ten thousand that we gave them, they would match it and train one dog. They used Labradors almost exclusively and they used poodles as well for their hypoallergenic qualities.

These dogs were trained to be full-time service dogs. If their handler suffered a seizure while walking or crossing the road, they would bark like crazy for help and also drag their handler out of harm's way. If the seizure happened indoors, they were trained to push a big red button to call 911 or EMS. We have little doubt that a seizure response dog would have saved Caroline's life. However, given her inability to alter her lifestyle, she never would have accepted such a restraint on her behaviour.

Approximately one-third of these dogs sensed a seizure about to happen and could get their handler out of harm's way. One such dog was Vader, who we sponsored for a lovely young school teacher whose seizures had worsened after an automobile accident. In class, he would grab her pant leg and force her to sit down before a seizure. This happened several times and she was unharmed. On another occasion, she was walking along the sidewalk of a busy street and Vader took her by the arm and dragged her away from the traffic and onto some soft grass so she would not harm herself. The best story was when she experienced a grand mal seizure and fell headfirst into a snowbank. Vader barked like crazy. No one came to her rescue, so Vader saved her life by dragging her out of the snowbank!

We sponsored Scooby for a ten-year-old boy who suffered from both epilepsy and autism. Lo and behold, his seizures stopped and he has not had one in ten years! Children with autism do not make friends easily but now he had a friend and constant companion. Clearly, his anxiety level went down significantly.

We became the single largest donor to the Lions Foundation Seizure Response Guide Dog Program, donating some $270,000 dollars to raise twenty-seven dogs. We would attempt to be at each graduation night to meet the recipients of the dogs. We have stayed in touch with many of these families.

There are many other heart-warming stories but, with these dogs, we fulfilled the Care-Alive mission of caring for those who are living.

Caroline would like that.

In addition, with our name spreading throughout the world of epilepsy, people reached out to us. One group represented children with epilepsy in the Hamilton Peel region. They have expanded since and are now the Epilepsy Association for South Central Ontario (ESCO). We liked them. They needed twenty thousand dollars to send kids to summer camp. They had raised a portion of that amount but asked us to fund the difference. We agreed to do that so twenty-four children could enjoy a two-week vacation where they had one-on-one counselling. This was because many of them had daily seizures and needed a constant expert companion. Not only was it a good break for the children, but their parents also got a break from their constant caregiving. Some of us would attend the picnic at the end of the vacation. It was heartwarming to say the least. We strengthened our bond with them, particularly after Cynthia Milbourn became in charge, and we supported them year after year.

Caroline would like that.

Also, we ran the charity softball tournament every year, raising approximately thirty thousand dollars each time. Most of the players knew nothing about Care-Alive and what we did. Thus, we invited a trainer with a response dog from the Lions Foundation to the tournament so the players could understand where their money was going.

Seizure Dog Recipients

Caroline was known to party some, and the head trader for Griffiths, the legendary Mike Wekerle, adored her. They were frequent dance partners at GMP's boat cruise and Christmas parties. Besides our own fundraising efforts, we were thrilled when the same Mike Wekerle donated one hundred thousand dollars to us. This allowed us to establish our early initiatives.

The foundation accomplished more: it brought together the Cunningham family as well as the legions upon legions of CC's friends. We worked shoulder-to-shoulder on ambitious fundraisers – ambitious for a volunteer group – and we succeeded. Our bond is now strong and life-long. This was even more important than the accomplishments of the foundation. Too many families disintegrate after similar tragedies. After the initial and horrific shock, we gathered around the cause and made a difference.

As we wound down foundation, partly owing to volunteer fatigue and partly because we felt a sense of accomplishment, we wanted to ensure that Caroline's name will endure. With our remaining funds, we discussed our options. We had been close to the Epilepsy South Central Ontario (ESCO) Society, managed brilliantly by Cynthia Melbourn. She proposed naming a teen drop-in centre in Caroline's name at their new Mississauga headquarters. We donated fifty thousand dollars and her name is on that centre.

We had been close to Toronto SickKids and Dr. Elizabeth Donner in particular. For one hundred thousand, we launched the Caroline Cunningham endowment, funds from which will go towards neurological education. We will add to this endowment and others will also.

We are so proud of these two dedications.

We have made a difference.

My conclusion, after contemplating all our efforts to save and improve lives, is that the net effect was to bring our family and close friends closer together in a united fashion. We did not fall apart. We rallied, and I believe that this rallying point was worth more than the actual stated purpose of the foundation.

Purple Day

In 2008, a nine-year-old schoolgirl in Nova Scotia, Cassidy Megan, an epilepsy sufferer, decided to promote a day for awareness for epilepsy. Her efforts went viral and March 26 became PURPLE DAY, an international day to draw attention to, and increase awareness of, epilepsy. She is now the International Spokesperson for Purple Day. One year we flew Cassidy and her mother, Angela McCarthy, to Toronto on Purple Day where she pushed the opening buzzer for the Toronto Stock Exchange, did a TV interview, attended different Purple Day activities, and watched with pride as the CN Tower turned purple. Valerie's interview of Cassidy can be viewed here: https://youtube/_50NIiHFOI8

Care-Alive decided to do something to bring more awareness by launching our own Purple Day initiative. Through my friendship with Eric Sinclair, the head of the TSX's

CN Tower Turns Purple

Cassidy Megan opens the TSX

Datalinx operation, we were able to open the Toronto Stock Exchange on nine consecutive Purple Days. Eric explained to me that charitable organizations could do this but would take second fiddle to corporations going public at the same time. Eric was also involved in the TSX donations committee and secured an annual donation of ten thousand dollars to Care-Alive. Eric loved the seizure response dogs and later, after moving on from the TSX, he sponsored a dog personally.

Opening the TSX, a nationally televised event, was a huge boost for awareness about epilepsy. We all dressed in purple to heighten the effect. We were also able to attract some prominent people to push the buzzer. Cassidy Megan herself pushed the buzzer one year.

Besides Cassidy, we were honoured by the participation of such notables as two-time Olympic Trampoline Champion Rosie MacLennan; J. Lyman Macinnis, my friend and long-time mentor; my granddaughter Charlie; a seizure response dog; Debi Hewson, CEO of Odlum Brown; and Julie Jelinek of Lions Foundation Dog Guides. Jeremy Fleming and Cynthia Melbourn of Epilepsy South Central Ontario were also on hand at the different openings.

I was a frequent guest on the Business News Network. The morning host, Frances Horedelski, was sympathetic to our cause and granted me a ten-minute interview just after the market opened. This generated even more publicity.

Other Fundraising Efforts

We became the charity of record for the annual Bay Street slo-pitch tournament through Tannis' friendship with the league president.

We raised approximately thirty thousand dollars per annum and, naturally, entered our own team, the CC Cosmos. We did not win but we had fun. Tannis did all the heavy lifting but everyone pitched in, including many volunteers.

The players had no idea what Care-Alive was about, apart from the GMP team, so we brought in a handler from the Lions Foundation with two seizure response dogs. She held demonstrations between games and thus the players had a better idea where their funds were going. They also learned that Caroline was a Bay Streeter and a keen softball player herself. Thus, our annual revenue rose each year.

However, similar to our Oscar party, hosting this tournament took its toll on all of us and it became harder to attract volunteers. Thus, we eventually ended our relationship with the tournament.

Cycling

I have been an avid cyclist for a long time, travelling the world on various trips. It seemed natural then to raise funds for Care-Alive via cycling as it would not take much planning and organization. This was successful. For three years I was joined by my wonderful friend Marketa Schusterova, who not only joined me on the one-hundred-kilometre ride but also raised a

With Marketa Schusterova

significant amount of funds. We raised a total of sixty thousand dollars through our rides with minimal time required. Besides Marketa's contributions, I received donations from my long-time supporters Debi Hewson, CEO of Odlum Brown; Peter McRae, Chairman of Freedom International; and Peter Conroy of Shorcan, to name just a few.

Charity Goes On

As it happened, our charitable work did not stop at our foundation. As an example, Caroline saw village after village in Africa where there were no fresh water wells and children (mostly girls) had to walk miles every day to obtain water (not drinkable fresh water) while encountering various risks.

Along with several friends from the Keg Restaurant, and initiated by Anna-Maria Sparks, we raised eight thousand dollars to fund the drilling of one fresh water well in a small village which Caroline had visited.

In addition, while in another village, she noticed children playing with new soccer balls and nets. She learned that an organization, Right To Play, a Canadian charity, donated all kinds of equipment to children in poor parts of the world.

Immediately, Caroline adopted it as her preferred charity and instructed her friends and family not to give her presents any more but to donate to this wonderful charity.

A fresh water well in Africa

Some of us have participated in the Lions Foundation Purina Walk and will continue to do so. Also, we have forged a strong bond with Toronto SickKids Hospital. Besides adding to Caroline's endowment, we will contribute to their massive expansion. For my part, I will continue to cycle to raise funds for the Lions Foundation, SickKids, and Caroline's endowment.

Thus, we have not stopped giving just because we dissolved our foundation. Caroline would like this as she had the most generous heart and spirit of anyone that I have ever known.

Memorials

For eleven consecutive years, we have honoured Caroline with a memorial in *The Globe and Mail.*

I wrote the first one, just after her death.

Suddenly, at age 32. Combining a zest for life with unbridled generosity and loyalty, Caroline, or "C.C." as she was affectionately known by her myriad of diverse friends, touched everyone. Besides her personal generosity to others, she gave liberally to many worthy causes. She had a natural curiosity which led her to adventures in the four corners of the world and she would try anything once. She was also passionate about the arts, loving everything from film festivals, to Broadway, to live concerts of all kinds. She is survived by her loving parents Kathleen and Hank and her beloved sister Valerie.

Following are examples of the annual memorial we published in *The Globe and Mail* every April 8:

April 8, 2012

You can shed tears that she is gone, or
You can smile because she lived.
You can close your eyes and pray that she will come back, or
You can open your eyes and see all that she left.
Your heart can be empty because you can't see her, or
You can be full of the love you shared with her.
You can turn your back on tomorrow and live yesterday, or

You can be happy for tomorrow because of yesterday.
You can remember her, and only that she is gone, or
You can cherish her memory and let it live on.
You can cry and close your mind, be empty, and turn your back, or
You can do what she would want:
Smile, open your eyes, love, and go on.
And so,
Of all that life has offered, and all that's left to do,
We will never have a greater gift than the years we spent with you.

APRIL 8, 2016

In Loving Memory
Dear Caroline
We remember you today
-Your zest for life
-Your radiating energy
-Your infectious laughter
-Your ever-present smile
-Your legendary hugs
-Your fierce love
Because of you we saw how one person could light up the world.
How we miss your presence in our lives.

April 8, 2017

"A Face Among the Stars" by Rebecca Ginns
I looked for you this morning
I looked for you last night
I looked for you everywhere but you were not in sight
I looked up to the sky above
And saw your face in the stars.
It was then I realized,
You're not here anymore
But you'll always be with me...
You will always be in my heart.
Life is something all of us must borrow

Returning it in time, to whence it came.
Goodbye doesn't mean you're gone. So long as I still love you
Your memory will live on.

April 8, 2018

Ten years, it is hard to believe.
Yet, we feel that she is still here.
She never left us.

Other Grief Thoughts

In the first few years, it was difficult. I am an emotional guy to start with. Occasionally I would watch the service and cry uncontrollably. "Feels like Home" always got to me. It was impossible to talk about it with anyone and it definitely altered my relationships as I was loath to bring the subject up.

Chapter 6

Moving On

I mentioned earlier that some of the healing process occurs in stages: as time has gone on, my anger level has subsided and my acceptance level has risen. She is not coming back. The years seem like a blur now. The first few were full of raw emotion and tears. I used to watch the service frequently, a guaranteed waterfall. I found it almost impossible to enter into any relationships. Gradually, I improved, but the emotions remained so close to the surface that it did not take much to set me off.

To be sure, I had lots of black days when I did not leave my house; I would break into tears at the slightest provocation. To be sure, I drank to excess at different times. These were futile attempts to "drown my sorrows." Sadly, alcohol is nothing but a short-term cure as it is ultimately a depressant. However, at no time did I ever contemplate harming myself.

The Cunninghams are survivors; they emigrated from Scotland in 1763 aboard a rickety ship called the Hector and carved out an existence in Stellarton, Nova Scotia. My father took over the dairy farm from his elderly father but was unable to make a go of it. He moved his young family to Toronto where he managed somehow to provide food and shelter for his six children. We Cunninghams possess a strong work ethic and a quiet pride in our accomplishments. Above all else, we have a stubborn streak (not always a positive!) which has helped us endure various hardships. We are survivors. At my core, I believed that we could do something positive after Caroline died. That led to the creation of our foundation and all the good things we accomplished in her name.

Eventually, as you have read, I rallied family and friends to bring us together in honouring Caroline. I am so proud of what a small but determined group of people can achieve.

Nevertheless, it was not easy. My professional career suffered.

I have been in and around the investment business for my whole career. A big percentage of my fifty-plus years on Bay Street has been as a bond trader. The bond trading community features enormous trading volumes; in my time, trillions of dollars of bonds were traded on verbal handshakes with nary an argument. It was, and is, an environment of honour and integrity. Bond traders were not only competitors, seeking to maximize business with customers, but they were also friends and allies as there was a mutual need for one another as counterparties. At one point, I was a significant factor in the institutional world: once as a zero-coupon expert at Gordon Capital and then as a Global Bond trader for CIBC. Since 1988, I built three more trading desks from scratch, specializing in the retail fixed income business. As a trader, for small investment dealers, but one running my own book of business, I needed the goodwill of the big traders on Bay Street, such as the chartered banks and other big investment dealers.

Friends

At the time of Caroline's death, I was managing yet another fixed income trading desk – this time for Blackmont Capital. It had been a bad decision to go there in the first place but I persevered and built a successful desk, which included two of Caroline's best friends (I realize there is no shortage of them): Nataly Alves and Jamie Price.

I was dispirited after CC died. Then came the 2008 meltdown in markets. CI, who had purchased Blackmont, declared me redundant and wrote me a cheque. I was floundering for months when I reconnected with Debi Hewson, the CEO of Odlum Brown, a successful Vancouver-based retail brokerage firm.

We became fast friends in the early 1990s. I was managing First Marathon's bond trading desk for its nascent Correspondent Network. I had several clients in Vancouver and I reconnected with Debi on one of my trips to Vancouver. We had met a few years prior when I gave my fearless forecast at the Vancouver CFA Annual Forecast dinner.

We stayed in touch and, although Odlum Brown was not a client, there was no reason to not provide them my services. Debi had moved from Dominion Securities to Odlum and was in charge of Odlum's bond and money market trading.

She thought that the Street was overcharging her and asked me to provide her with offerings. I did so in an innovative electronic fashion (this was the early nineties!) and we began to do business together. Our friendship grew and we stayed in touch.

We met in Toronto after my demise from Blackmont and she asked me if I was interested in joining Odlum Brown. I was interested and I joined Odlum on April 1, 2009 and I am still there today.

Debi knew me well and knew how much I loved my children. Since joining Odlum she has been nothing but totally supportive. When I launched my foundation, she supported all my fundraising initiatives financially, she attended an Oscar Night fundraiser, and she opened the TSX on Purple Day. We froze our buns off that day while we watched the CN Tower turn purple!

She maintains this attitude and approach constantly. She will never know how much her support has meant to me, but I will say that I am fortunate to be the recipient of her big-hearted generosity and love.

Another person who has been there for me through everything for over thirty-four years is Stephen Reid. We met at a gymnastics meet in Oakville and the two of us ran the Oakville Antoinettes successfully for many years. He moved to Hastings, ten minutes from me, after marrying Patricia Connor, whose family is from nearby Campbellford. He knew my daughters well as two of his four daughters were close in age to Caroline and Valerie. Since Caroline's passing, he has been a constant in my life, always there anytime I needed to talk. He would seldom let three days go by without phoning and checking in on me. My friendship with Steve is an anchor for me. He has always been willing to listen to me. He knew Caroline well and thus could reminisce and commiserate with me.

Charlie

A major turning point in my life occurred on August 25, 2012.

Valerie and Vincent Rother were married at my country house in Hastings in a beautiful outdoor ceremony. As a result of this union, Charlie Jessica Rother entered the world on November 20, 2013.

After losing a child, I adopted certain principles of Buddhism and the continuum of life. We live on through others. The arrival of Charlie has been an absolute and relative blessing. Caroline lives on through her. Not only has this kept me sane, but also it has helped me to shift my focus.

What a child she is! She combines intelligence, athleticism, and precociousness with an amazing amount of empathy rarely seen in anyone, never mind one so young.

Of course, I do not see her enough, but that does not matter so much. Just knowing that she is out there, dazzling everyone with her sociability and intelligence, is plenty for me.

So, on her own, she is fantastic. I certainly had no idea what it would be like to be a grandfather but, based on this sample, it is a marvelous thing.

On the grief side, she has, without doubt, accelerated my improved mental status and added to my happiness.

On another related note, we had preserved Caroline's room almost as a shrine with all her chosen antique furniture and her golf clubs, tennis racquet, boomerang, blanket from Africa, ukulele, etc.

Well, another big positive was to convert Caroline's room to become Charlie's room with new modern furniture and a funky bed. This change has brightened my house considerably, adding a huge element of happiness and removing the less-than-joyous atmosphere of the shrine to Caroline.

She has also been responsible for a revival in my desire to celebrate special occasions. It is wondrous to watch her embrace Christmas, Thanksgiving, and even Easter. She has gradually become aware that her mother had a sister once; she accompanies us to CC's tree in Toronto every April 8.

I look forward to each and every time I get to spend time with her. Around her, I am very calm and internally happy.

Apart from my improved mental state and happiness, I have made a determined effort to remain as fit and healthy as possible. I would love to see her grow up.

Summary

"We are a continuum. Just as we reach back to our ancestors for our fundamental values, so we, as guardians of that legacy, must reach ahead to our children and their children and we do so with a sense of sacredness in that reaching."

Paul Tsongas

Most books end with a conclusion. This one does not.

We have been on this uncharted journey without GPS since April 8, 2007. Without such aid, we have stumbled our way through starts and stops, triumphs and defeats, hopes and despair. I have an idea what early explorers felt like as they set out for unknown destinations.

I can look back now and see the waypoints on this path: the early blurred years, the forming of Care-Alive and the successful fundraising and the lives we saved, the coming together and unification of not only my family, but CC's legions of friends.

To be sure, we went down some blind alleys, had successes and failures, and tears and laughter.

Valerie's wedding and the subsequent arrival of the wonderful Charlie was a significant waypoint. Also, we resumed celebration of major holidays, particularly Christmas. However, Easter will never be the same.

The healing process continued, with the tenth anniversary celebration being a major turning point in my life. I declared myself healed after then.

This healing led to the thought of writing this book as a tribute to her and as a guide for others. I could not have contemplated writing it until I was sufficiently healed. We have all changed and we have survived this journey largely intact. Our lives go on and we will encounter more waypoints. We can see more clearly now, and we are better equipped to handle what comes our way.

This book is meant to be my eulogy to Caroline. Writing it has brought me more freedom and I feel that I have honoured her. We have ensured that her name will live on. No one will forget Caroline.

Caroline remains in all our thoughts at all times. We are delighted to have accomplished wonderful things in her name. While our goals are not as united and focused as they once were, nevertheless we intend to do our part, principally by making as substantial donations as possible to her endowment at Toronto SickKids hospital, the funds from which will go principally to assisting and educating those in the neurology world. This story is not complete. The fact that I have been able to write this much is a testimony to the healing process. Life goes on. Time goes by. People marry, have children, grow careers, and change priorities.

I remain in the investment business, working for the finest brokerage firm in Canada, Odlum Brown. I am maintaining a large property in rural Ontario, travelling the world, and will continue to write.

Kathleen is retired and living on Stoney Lake with Bill. She also likes to travel and has contributed to this book.

Valerie continues to grow her excellent career in human resources and employment. She is married to Vincent Rother, a man of many talents. Currently he is using them as a stuntman in the film industry. Valerie and Vincent are parents of course to their precocious six-year-old daughter, Charlie Jessica.

When one sees Charlie at her social and empathetic best, you know that Caroline is still alive.

Of course, there is no logical end to this story. We all continue to mend at our individual paces. We carry on, getting stronger.

One of the keys has been to avoid the "what-ifs."

This has been a significant item for me. I cannot change anything; I cannot bring her back. There can only be heartache and sleepless nights if I permit myself to wallow in self-recrimination or doubts on what I could have done differently.

No matter how much better we have become as time marches on, there is one overarching conclusion:

Grief never ends.

Appendix A

Finding the Paving Stones

1. Enter Central Park at East 67th Street. Make sure to enter from the east side.
2. Walk past a playground and a statue of Balto, the sled dog.
3. Walk under the road overpass.
4. You will emerge at the Mall (south end of Literary Walk).
5. If you see Shakespeare's statue, you are close.
6. Look for the facing statues of Rabbie Burns and Sir Walter Scott. They are just north of the stones.
7. The red stones are in the shape of a compass. Caroline's stone is in the northwest, facing Canada.

Finding the Tree

1. From her stone, walk north on Literary Walk to Bethesda Terrace and Fountain.
2. Bear right around the fountain and continue, passing a lake on the left and a restaurant (good spot for a glass of vino!). With the restaurant on the left, follow the path beside the road until you see a sign for Belvedere Castle.
3. Turn left towards the Castle and turn right shortly so that Turtle Pond will be on your left. You will pass the statue of Jaqiello, the Polish warrior king, on the right.
4. The tree is just ahead where the path intersects with the path crossing the south end of the Great Lawn. It is a red maple.
5. I have the coordinates as 40.46'47.73"N, 73. 58'01.35" W.

Appendix B

What is Sudden/Unexplained Death in Epilepsy?

Sudden unexplained death in epilepsy or SUDEP is the term used to describe when a person with epilepsy dies unexpectedly without a clear cause. The condition was first observed in 1854; however, a formal definition is still being debated today. Nashif (1997) presented one of the most widely accepted definitions within the scientific community, which is "the sudden, unexpected, witnessed or unwitnessed, non-traumatic, and non-drowning death in patients with epilepsy with or without evidence for a seizure, and excluding documented status epilepticus (a seizure lasting more than 30 minutes), in which post mortem examination does not reveal a structural or toxicological cause for death." [1,2] The main problem with this definition is that it requires a post-mortem autopsy, whose quality and timing vary considerably among countries. Furthermore, this definition may not be useful in epidemiological or statistical studies that attempt to understand why the condition occurs and to identify risks for SUDEP. Therefore, the Annegers' (1997) criteria are used in the absence of an autopsy for these types of studies. These are 1) a patient with epilepsy dies suddenly while in a reasonable state of health; 2) the death occurred within minutes; 3) the death occurred while performing normal, everyday duties; 4) no obvious cause of death was found; and 5) the death was not directly caused by a seizure or status epilepticus.[3,4] Regardless of the definition, for many who have epilepsy, their friends and family are not aware of the possibility of SUDEP until it is too late. Furthermore, the word "unexplained" in the definition points to the multitude of unknown factors surrounding this devastating event.

Risk Factors for Sudden Unexplained Death in Epilepsy

The reality is that epilepsy appears to be associated with a two-to-threefold increase in SUDEP compared to the general population and is the most common direct epilepsy-related cause of death.[5] Incidence rates are difficult to accurately ascertain because of a lack of post-mortem examinations; however, cohort studies, or a statistical study of a group of people who share common characteristics, have shown that SUDEP occurs in a range from approximately 1:100 person per year in intractable epilepsy surgery cohorts to 0.35/1,000 persons-years in an epilepsy population-based study.[6] From these studies, a number of risk factors have been observed.

I. Treatment with Anti-Epileptic Drugs (AEDs)

There are a number of factors involving AEDs that have been shown to increase the risk for SUDEP. One of the more apparent risks is the use of more than one medication at a time (polytherapy versus monotherapy) and frequent changes in medication.[6, 7] It is believed that this can affect the postictal state (the state of consciousness after a seizure) or cause a dysfunction in the body's autonomic system.[6] Another study showed that the number of AEDs taken over a lifetime or no treatment at all can also increase the risk for SUDEP.[8]

Lack of patient compliance to treatment protocols has been proposed as a risk factor; however, the results of studies have been mostly contradictory. This risk cannot be completely dismissed because accurate information about how medications were taken are not always available after death. Furthermore, post-mortem blood analysis may not accurately portray AED levels making it difficult to determine whether the patient was compliant.[6, 9] That being said, analysis of hair samples using high-performance liquid chromatography (HPLC) showed that there was an increased variability in AED concentrations in SUDEP patients.[10] In addition, almost all of these studies attempting to resolve this issue have been based on three AEDs ¾ pheytoin, carbamazephine and lamotrigine. Despite this controversy, patient compliance is important to overall patient health, especially those living with epilepsy. Subtherapeutic drug levels, or taking doses that are too low to be therapeutic, is one of the strongest risk factors for SUDEP.

Finally, whether certain AEDs provide a higher risk for SUDEP has also been evaluated. Some studies have shown that there is no AED in particular that increases the SUDEP risk, while others have impliedthat higher than normal levels of certain drugs may elevate risk.[6, 7, 8, 17, 18, 18, 28] All in all, the studies have been largely contradictory. That being said, it is obviously important that using AEDs aggressively, causing blood concentrations to be above therapeutic levels (as well as below), should be generally avoided regardless of the AED used. It is clearly important to follow prescription schedules.

II. Age, Gender, and Ethnicity

The age at the highest risk for SUDEP appears to be between the ages of 20 and 40 years old.[11, 12, 13] Ficker et al. (1998) reported that seven out of the nine SUDEP cases assessed were within the ages of 15 and 44.[13] However, there are reported SUDEP cases of people from anywhere between the ages of 8 months to 83 years.[9] Unfortunately, many of these cohort studies are fraught with bias, but the accepted wisdom appears to be that people are at a higher risk for SUDEP within the ages of 20 to 40, especially those with poor seizure control.[11, 12] SUDEP in children is often overlooked; however, an important Ontario study assessing 27 cases under 15 years of age showed an incidence of 1-2 deaths per 10,000 patients-years.[14, 15]

Conclusions about gender and ethnicity as they relate to SUDEP risk are equally biased. Some cohorts reveal that men are more susceptible, others reveal that women are more susceptible, but most show that gender does not contribute to risk.[8, 9, 14, 16] Finally, a number of studies have demonstrated that people of African descent have a higher incidence of SUDEP; however, the selection of patients within the cohort is biased as well as a number of confounding factors were ignored.[9]

III. Types of Seizures, Remission, and Age of Onset

Patients who have refractory seizures have the highest risk for SUDEP.[11, 17, 19] It is believed that 10-50% of SUDEP cases are within this category.[9] Refractory epilepsy is a multi-faceted condition and experts tend to group individuals who have not had seizure control for over 18 months and whose treatment regimens with two or more different AEDs have failed.[20, 21] This would help to explain some of the risks related to AED treatment discussed earlier. Many studies have shown that the incidence of SUDEP is inversely related to remission of epilepsy, and the MRC Antiepileptic drug withdrawal study has confirmed that the SUDEP is rare in patients in remission.[9, 22] This means that proper seizure control is key and it is imperative to find proper medication as soon as possible in order to reduce the risk of SUDEP. In addition, it appears that people who experience generalized tonic-clonic (sometimes called "grand mal") seizures especially if experienced within the past year are susceptible.[6, 8, 9, 11, 23] Seizure frequency, especially generalized tonic clonic seizures, is probably the strongest risk factor for SUDEP and deaths have occurred in patients with as few as one to three seizures within a year.[7, 16] Finally, it appears that all types of epilepsy (idiopathic, cryptogenic, symptomatic, and unclassified) experience deaths from SUDEP; however, the symptomatic epilepsy group (those with an identifiable cause for epilepsy) had the most deaths within 10 years from diagnosis.[12]

Those diagnosed with chronic epilepsy in childhood are at the highest risk for SUDEP, especially when they are under the age of 20.[9,12] Furthermore, the statistical models showed increased mortality with rising age in patients with chronic epilepsy, especially those living with epilepsy for 15-20 years.[9, 12] Another at-risk group appears to be those newly diagnosed in adulthood (median age of 29 years).[12] The SUDEP cases within this group occurred mostly between the ages of 31-40.[12] The studies showed that the incidence of SUDEP increased more than 42% in patients with newly diagnosed epilepsy wherein any of the AEDs prescribed were unable to control seizures.[12] This is yet another reason why seizure control is incredibly important.

IV. Epilepsy with other Neurological Problems

Mental retardation (IQ<70) along with a seizure disorder accounts for up to 45% of SUDEP cases.[9] However, again, studies have been contradictory, but it is still considered a risk factor even after adjusting for seizure frequency.[9, 16] Regardless, the evidence is weak. Other neurological disorders that have also shown contradictory results include the use of psychotropic drugs along with AEDs and the development of brain lesions. The concurrent use of psychotropic drugs has a very weak relationship to SUDEP.[16] One study showed that focal CNS lesions were reported in 35-50% of SUDEP cases within a study group; however, these are not supported by other case-controlled studies.[9]

V. Lifestyle Factors

Drinking alcohol is often an issue with treatment of many neurological disorders. This is because alcohol can easily cross the blood brain barrier and possibly disrupt the passage of AEDs, thereby leading to poor seizure control. Although this appears to be a simple explanation, in reality it is very complex and the relation between alcoholism and SUDEP is very weak.[9, 24]

There is a perpetuating myth that physical activity can induce seizures and increase their frequency.[25] In fact, exercise-related seizures are rare and better fitness can improve cardiovascular and psychological health.[25] A surprising case study exists of a 33-year-old active duty soldier who survived the events leading to SUDEP before collapsing in the midst of rigorous training.[26] Although this could be construed as a risk factor, it may be more likely due to the dehydration, electrolyte imbalance, hyperventilation, and hyperthermia that can occur during exercise and are known to increase the likelihood of seizures.[26] What can be learned from this is that physical activity should be within normal levels. Finally, care should be taken to minimize the above during physical activity.

VI. Respiratory, Cardiac, and Genetic Mechanisms

Pulmonary edema or the fluid build-up in the lungs that can lead to respiratory failure has been found in a large number of SUDEP cases.[6] Most unwitnessed SUDEP cases occur in bed and 71% are found in the prone sleeping position.[6] This position, a common cause of Sudden Infant Death Syndrome (SIDS), results in respiratory obstruction. In addition, sleep apnoea or snoring is associated with seizures, which may attribute to respiratory issues that can lead to SUDEP.[27]

Possible cardiac mechanisms in SUDEP are hypothetical and include possible primary or secondary cardiac mechanisms.[6] There may be certain people who are mildly predisposed to SUDEP because of various cardiac disorders, and uncontrolled seizure control could heighten the risk.[6] Genetic susceptibility is currently being studied. In particular, defects in potassium channel genes, sodium channel genes, genes that cause long-QT syndrome, H-Channel genes, and calcium signalling genes may have roles in causing SUDEP.[6]

VII. Other Possible Preventive Measures

Obviously, the main goal to reduce the likelihood of SUDEP is proper seizure control; however, the AEDs have limited clinical efficacy in about one third of patients.[5] Since genetic, environmental and social factors could contribute to the lack of efficacy, non-medical and surgical preventative measures may reduce the risk of SUDEP.[5] First, increased omega-3 fatty acids (3000-to 4,000 mg of daily fish oil supplements or 2-3 servings of fish) have a number of health benefits, but it is the prevention of cardiac arrhythmias and sudden cardiac death that make this helpful in reducing the SUDEP risk. Another suggestion would be to increase physical activity to improve overall cardiovascular health because some of the mechanisms behind SUDEP that have been proposed include autonomic effects such as cardiovascular disturbances.[5] Physical activity is also considered to have anticonvulsant effects. The risk of SUDEP appears to increase in very cold winter seasons.[5,14]

Summary and Conclusion

These studies have shown a number of risk factors that may lead to SUDEP. Some of the risks mentioned were weakly correlated with SUDEP while others were very strongly correlated and provide substantial motivation for those with epilepsy to reduce the possibility of SUDEP. Seizure control is of utmost importance and there needs to be more research in developing future AEDS to control seizures, especially generalized tonic clonic seizures. Another element that needs to be addressed is better screening for determining what kind of AEDS would be effective right away rather than approaching treatment in a trial and error fashion, thereby minimizing the overall number of AEDs used. The population most affected (i.e. chronic epilepsy diagnosed in childhood and newly diagnosed in adulthood [mean age of 29]) need to be especially cautious. Finally, lifestyle choices play a role because reducing sleep apnoea, avoiding the prone sleeping position, eating plenty of healthy fats versus a diet high in saturated fats (i.e. Omega-3 fatty acids), and exercise could also substantially reduce SUDEP cases.

Written by Kimberly Berman, BSc
June 16, 2009

References

1. Nashef, L. (1997). *Sudden Unexplained Death from Epilepsy: Terminology and Definition.* Epilepsia; 38:S6-S8.
2. Huff, J. (2007). *Status Epilepticus*. Emedicine; http://emedicine.medscape.com/article/793708-overview
3. Annegers, J. (1997). *United States Perspective on Definitions and Classifications: International Workshop on Epilepsy and Sudden Death*. Epilepsia; 38(S11):S9-S12.
4. Tomson, T., Walczak, T., Sillanpaa, M., and Sander, J. (2005). *Sudden Unexpected Death in Epilepsy: A Review of Incidence and Risk Factors.* Epilepsia; 46(11):54-61.
5. Scorza, F., Colugnati, D., Pansani, A., Sonoda, E., Arida, R., and Cavalheiro, E. (2008). *Preventing Tomorrow's Sudden Cardiac Death in Epilepsy: What Should Physicians Know About This?* Clinics; 63:389-94.
6. Nashef, L., Hindocka, N., and Makoff, A. (2007). *Risk Factors in Sudden Death Epilepsy (SUDEP): The Quest for Mechanisms.* Epilepsia; 48(5):859-871.
7. Nilsson, L., Farahmand, B., Persson, P., Thilbin, I., and Tomson, T. (1999). *Risk Factors for Sudden Unexplained Death in Epilepsy: A Case Control Study.* The Lancet; 353:888-893.
8. Langan, Y. Nashef, L., and Sander, J. (2005). *Case-Control Study of SUDEP.* Neurology; 34: 1131-33.
9. Tomson, T., Skold, A., Holmgen, P., Nilsson, L., and Danielsson, B. (1998). *Postmortem Changes in Blood Concentrations of Phenytoin and Carbamazepine: An Experimental Study.* Therapeutic Drug Monitoring; 20(3):309-12.
10. Williams, J., Lawthom, C., Dunstan, F., Dawson, T., Kerr, M., Wilson, J., and Smith, P. (2006). *Variability of Antiepileptic Medication Taking Behavior in*

Sudden Unexplained Death in Epilepsy: Hair Analysis at Autopsy. J Neurol Neurosurg Psychiatry; 77:481-84.

11. Hitris, N., Suratman, K., Stephen, L., Sills, G., and Brodie, M. (2007). *Sudden Unexplained Death in Epilepsy: A Search for Risk Factors.* Epilepsy & Behavior; 10(1):138-41.
12. Mohanraj, R., Norrie, J., Stephen, L., Kelly, K., Hitris, N., and Brodie, M. (2006). *Mortality in Adults with Newly Diagnosed and Chronic Epilepsy: A Retrospective Comparative Study.* The Lancet Neurology; 5:481-87.
13. Ficker, D., So, E., Shen, W., Annegers, J., O'Brien, P., Cascino, G., and Belau, P. (1998). *Population-based Study of the Incidence of Sudden Unexplained Death from Epilepsy.* Neurology; 51:1270-74.
14. So, E. (2006). *Demystifying Sudden Unexplained Death in Epilepsy – Are We Close?* Epilepsia; 47(S7):87-92.
15. Donner, E., Smith, C., and Snead, C. (2001). *Sudden Unexplained Death in Children with Epilepsy.* Neurology; 57:430-434.
16. Walczak, T., Leppik, L., D'Amelio, M., Rarick, J., So, E., Ahman, P., Ruggles, K., Cascino, G., Annegers, J., and Hauser, W. (2001). *Incidence and Risk Factors in Sudden Unexplained Death in Epilepsy: A Prospective Cohort Study.* Neurology; 56:519-25.
17. Nilsson, L., Bergman, U., Diwan, V., Farahmand, Persson, P., and Tomson, T. (2001). *Antiepileptic Drug Therapy and Its Management in Sudden Unexpected Death in Epilepsy: A Case-Control Study.* Epilepsia; 42(5):667-673.
18. So, J. (2008). *What is Known about the Mechanisms Underlying SUDEP?* Epilepsia; 49(S9):93-98.
19. Kloster, R. and Engelskjon, T. (1999). *Sudden Unexplained Death in Epilepsy (SUDEP): A Clinical Perspective and a Search for Risk Factors.* J Neurol Neurosurg Psychiatry; 67:439-444.
20. Berg, A., Vickrey, B., Testa, F., Levy, S., Shinnar, S., DiMario, F., and Smith, S. (2006). *How Long Does it Take for Epilepsy to Become Intractable? A Prospective Investigation.* Annals of Neurology; 60(1):73-79.
21. French, J. (2007). *Refractory Epilepsy: Clinical Overview.* Epilepsia; 48(S1):3-7.
22. Medical Research Council (1991). *Randomized Study of Antiepileptic Drug Withdrawal in Patients in Remission.* The Lancet; 337:1175-1180.
23. Monte, C., Arends, J., Tan, I., Aledenkamp, A., Limburg, M., and de Krom, M. (2007). *Sudden Unexplained Death from Epilepsy.* Seizure; 16:1-7.

24. Tellez-Zenteno, J., Ronquillo, L., and Wiebe, S. (2005). *Sudden Unexpected Death from Epilepsy: Evidence-based Analysis of Incidence and Risk Factors.* Epilepsy Research; 65:101-115.
25. Arida, R., Cavalheiro, E., da Silva, A., and Scorza, F. (2008). *Physical Activity and Epilepsy: Proven and Predicted Benefits.* Sports Medicine; 38(7):607-615.
26. Harrison, B. and Asplund, C. (2007). *Sudden Unexplained Death in Epilepsy During Physical Activity.* Current Sports Medicine Reports; 6:13-15.
27. Nashef, L., Walker, F., Allen, P., Sander, J., Shorvan, S., and Fish, D. (1996). *Apnoea and Bradycardia During Epileptic Seizures: Relation to SUDEP.* Journal of Neurology, Neurosurgery, and Psychiatry; 60:297-300.
28. Opeskin, K., Burke, M., Cordner, S., and Berkovic, S. (1999). *Comparison of Antiepileptic Drug Levels in Sudden Unexplained Deaths in Epilepsy with Deaths from Other Causes.* Epilepsia; 40(12):1795-98.